COLLEGE STUDY

third edition
COLLEGE STUDY
the essential ingredients

SALLY A. LIPSKY
Indiana University of Pennsylvania

PEARSON

Boston   Columbus   Indianapolis   New York   San Francisco   Upper Saddle River
Amsterdam   Cape Town   Dubai   London   Madrid   Milan   Munich   Paris   Montréal   Toronto
Delhi   Mexico City   São Paulo   Sydney   Hong Kong   Seoul   Singapore   Taipei   Tokyo

Editor-in-Chief: Jodi McPherson
Editor: Katie Mahan
Editorial Assistant: Clara Ciminelli
Executive Marketing Manager: Amy Judd
Production Editor: Annette Joseph
Manufacturing Buyer: Megan Cochran
Interior Design, Electronic Composition,
   and Editorial Production Service: Integra
Photo Researcher: Annie Fuller
Cover Designer: Diane Lorenzo

Library of Congress Cataloging-in-Publication Data

Lipsky, Sally A.
   College study: the essential ingredients/Sally A. Lipsky.—3rd ed.
      p. cm.
   Includes bibliographical references and index.
   ISBN 978-0-13-218089-4
1. Study skills.   2. Critical thinking—Study and teaching (Higher)   I. Title.
   LB2395.L49 2013
   378.1'70281—dc23

                                                    2012001185

10 9 8 7 6 5 4 3 2 1

ISBN-13: 978-0-13-218089-4
ISBN-10: 0-13-218089-8

*In loving memory
of Irene and Merle*

About the Author

Upon graduation from the University of New Mexico (B.S. elementary education), Sally Lipsky began her career as a Title I reading instructor with the Houston (TX) public school district. After earning an M.Ed. in reading education from Texas Southern University, she taught in the Pittsburgh (PA) public schools. She earned a Ph.D. in language communications and adult education from the University of Pittsburgh and continued her career at Indiana University of Pennsylvania, where she has worked for over 20 years as a faculty member in the Developmental Studies Department, College of Education and Educational Technology. Her work has centered on aspects of student learning at the post-secondary level, including college reading and study strategies and peer-to-peer academic support. She is a long-time member of the College Reading and Learning Association (CRLA) and the National Association for Developmental Education (NADE), and has made numerous professional presentations. She authored the text *A Training Guide for College Tutors and Peer Educators*, published by Pearson Education, 2011.

Brief Contents

Contents

Chapter 3

MAXIMIZING YOUR PRODUCTIVITY   35

Chapter 4

ACTIVE LISTENING AND NOTE TAKING   49

Chapter 5

READING AND STUDYING TEXT MATERIAL   75

Chapter 6

ENHANCING YOUR LEARNING AND MEMORY   103

Chapter 7

PREPARING FOR TESTS   117

Chapter 8

TAKING TESTS   137

Chapter 9

CONTINUING YOUR ACADEMIC SUCCESS: A REVIEW   155

INDEX   159

Preface

This text provides a complete and balanced coverage of essential learning and study techniques at the post-secondary level. The author employs an active learning approach—the reader chooses, immediately applies, and then critiques practical strategies, with the goal of creating an effective, efficient, and individualized system of study. Content is presented to help students become self-regulating learners and problem solvers.

New to This Edition

Changes and updates are based on current research and literature as well as feedback from college instructors and students. In this text readers are exposed to *how* to make informed choices about learning content that is often new, complex, and changing rapidly, especially given the increasing link between technology and learning. Included is the inter-relationship of students' learning behaviors and attitudes, with an emphasis on applying multi-modal strategies to daily course work. The ultimate goal is for students to develop a personal system of study that works best for them.

- Technology updates:
  - Embedded within all chapters is information regarding the use of technology in college learning and studying. Also, new comments in **Student Voices** reflect the increasing use of technology in college academics.
  - The corresponding icon indicates added sections within chapters, titled **Online Course Work.** These sections contain information relating chapter topics to online, hybrid, and other Web-based course work.
- As indicated by the new title, **Enhancing Your Learning and Memory,** the content of Chapter 6 now emphasizes strategies to strengthen learning *and* memory. Research demonstrates the powerful effect of peer-to-peer

learning, thus the added section on collaborative learning and how to create study groups.

- Because of the large quantity of information, test-taking content is now divided into two chapters: **Preparing for Tests** (Chapter 7) and **Taking Tests** (Chapter 8). This separation should ease pacing of content and classroom presentation. Both chapters contain information about preparing for and taking online exams, and information on cumulative final exams has been added to Chapter 7.

- Strategies grouped according to visual, auditory, or tactile/kinesthetic learning modalities (as opposed to learning styles) are included in the **Try It Out!** and **Assess Your Success** exercises. Students identify, try out, and assess specific strategies, with the goal of developing multi-modal systems of study. (The switch from learning styles to modalities reflects current literature; matching learning styles and strategies appears to have a weak impact on student learning. Furthermore, incorporating a variety of sensory modalities seems to have a positive impact on learning and memory, especially for difficult subject matter.)

- As a means of reinforcing content through practice, application, and additional resources, the accompanying Instructor's Resource Manual includes information on **MyStudentSuccessLab,** Pearson Education's online product through which students have access to peer-led video presentations, interactive exercises, and projects. MyStudentSuccessLab presents information on these topics related to the text:

  - Time Management
  - Values/Goal Setting
  - Learning Preferences
  - Listening and Taking Notes in Class
  - Reading and Annotating
  - Memory and Studying
  - Problem Solving
  - Test-Taking Skills
  - Stress Management

Features

The text integrates three elements of how students learn:

1. *Strategies:* Covers important and practical study techniques that students can apply immediately in their daily academic courses.
2. *Attitude:* Provides opportunities for students to explore their levels of interest, motivation, and commitment toward transferring learning techniques to their day-to-day lives as college students.

3. *Learning modalities:* Students identify, implement, and evaluate specific visual, auditory, and tactile/kinesthetic learning and study strategies, with the goal of creating a successful system of study.

Additional features of the text include:

- Activities involving *critical, creative, or problem-solving thinking skills,* designated by the corresponding icon. Examples are analyzing academic behaviors and attitudes, critiquing why a strategy does or does not work, predicting and solving academic problems, differentiating types of test questions, and creating or modifying study aids that are most effective and efficient for the individual.
Critical Thinking Task
- *Comprehension checks* at the end of each chapter allow students to check their understanding and recall of key content.
- Streamlined format and an informal, personal writing style maintain *reader's attention.*
- Focus on *modeling* the essentials of learning helps readers apply strategies to course work. Illustrations of how peers apply specific strategies, in the form of visual examples and students' comments, provide both appealing and convincing models.
- Relevant activities immediately *engage* readers.

This text is intended for use in either a two-year or four-year institution within a variety of contexts:

- A study skills or learning strategies course
- A skills course linked or paired with content-area course work
- An introductory-level content course using a supplemental learning strategies text
- A first-year orientation program or seminar
- A series of workshops for first-year students or students on academic probation
- A tutor or peer educator training course requiring a college learning strategies text

For the Student: An Introduction to Text Features

AT THE BEGINNING OF CHAPTERS

- **Focus Questions.** Examine the focus questions when previewing the chapter. Then read to discover the answers to the questions. This strategy will help you become a more perceptive and involved reader.
- **Chapter Terms.** Review these key concepts before reading the chapter. When you have completed the chapter, check your understanding by providing both a meaning and an example for each term.

WITHIN CHAPTERS

- **Pause...and Reflect.** These exercises provide opportunities to think about and process key ideas. Questions will guide your observations and commentary. Your instructor may ask you to share your reflections as part of a group discussion or activity.
- **Models.** Illustrative examples within the text of how other college students applied strategies in a variety of courses can be used as templates for your own course work.
- **Student Voices.** Interspersed within chapters are compelling comments and tips from other college students. Reading about your peers' experiences and suggestions can help guide and motivate you to apply similar strategies.
- **Try It Out!** These exercises direct you to *apply* immediately a strategy introduced in the chapter, a crucial aspect of developing a personal system of study.
- **Assess Your Success.** After trying out a strategy, evaluate your performance by answering a series of questions.

Critical Thinking Task

- **Critical Thinking Tasks.** The corresponding icon indicates that a particular section or activity involves critical, creative, or problem-solving thinking skills.

- **Online Course Work.** The corresponding icon indicates information that relates chapter topics to online and hybrid courses and other Web-based learning situations.
- **Personal Action Statements.** You will choose specific strategies to implement within a designated time frame with the purpose of identifying which techniques do and do not work for you. Through the process of choosing, using, and assessing strategies you will work toward building an effective and efficient study system for yourself.

AT THE END OF CHAPTERS

- **Chapter Conclusions** provide a practical overview of the essential strategies and are a useful reference for future semesters.
- **Comprehension Checks** remind you to go back to the first page of each chapter and answer the focus questions and define the chapter terms or complete a similar summative activity.

NEW! COURSESMART ETEXTBOOK AVAILABLE

CourseSmart is an exciting new choice for students looking to save money. As an alternative to purchasing the printed textbook, students can purchase an electronic version of the same content. With a CourseSmart eTextbook, students can search the text, make notes online, print out reading assignments that incorporate lecture notes, and bookmark important passages for later review. For more information, or to purchase access to the CourseSmart eTextbook, visit www.coursesmart.com.

For the Instructor

An Instructor's Resource Manual accompanies the text and includes these features:

- Problem-solving scenarios centered on topics presented in the text, PowerPoint™ presentations for class instruction, and a course-culminating assignment from Chapter 9.
- Suggestions on how to use text features for in-class activities, including small-group collaborative work, journal writing, and group discussion.
- Five-point *chapter quizzes* that provide a modest check of students' comprehension; instructors may choose to use the quizzes as an extrinsic incentive for students to read assigned chapters.
- Pages to use for duplicating for students or projecting images to classes, including examples of note taking.
- Sample lesson plans for each chapter.
- A *sample syllabus*, including an outline of activities for a one-credit or two-credit college learning skills course.

Acknowledgments

I thank the following people for their professional reviews regarding this edition of the text: Christie Carr, Austin Community College; Debra DeMinck, Minnesota State University; Kyle Ellis, University of Mississippi; Howard Masuda, California State University; Katarina Moyon, Winthrop College; Janet Zupan, University of Montana, Missoula. Also, I thank my colleagues at Indiana University of Pennsylvania for their insightful and helpful comments about updates for the text.

Supplemental Resources

INSTRUCTOR SUPPORT – Resources to simplify your life and support your students.

Book Specific

Online Instructor's Manual – This manual is intended to give professors a framework or blueprint of ideas and suggestions that may assist them in providing their students with activities, journal writing, thought-provoking situations, and group activities. The test bank, organized by chapter includes: multiple choice, true/false and short-answer questions that support the key features in the book. This supplement is available for download from the Instructor's Resource Center at www.pearsonhighered.com/irc

Online PowerPoint Presentation – A comprehensive set of PowerPoint slides that can be used by instructors for class presentations or by students for lecture preview or review. The PowerPoint Presentation includes bullet point slides for each chapter, as well as all of the graphs and tables found in the textbook. These slides highlight the important points of each chapter to help students understand the concepts within each chapter. Instructors may download these PowerPoint presentations from the Instructor's Resource Center at www.pearsonhighered.com/irc

MyStudentSuccessLab – Are you teaching online, in a hybrid setting, or looking to infuse technology into your classroom for the first time? It is an online solution designed to help students build the skills they need to succeed for ongoing personal and professional development at www.mystudentsuccesslab.com

Other Resources

"Easy access to online, book-specific teaching support is now just a click away!"
Instructor Resource Center – Register. Redeem. Login. Three easy steps that open the door to a variety of print and media resources in downloadable, digital format, available to instructors exclusively through the Pearson 'IRC'. www.pearsonhighered.com/irc

"Provide information highlights on the most critical topics for student success!"
Success Tips is a 6-panel laminate with topics that include MyStudentSuccessLab, Time Management, Resources All Around You, Now You're Thinking, Maintaining Your Financial Sanity, and Building Your Professional Image. Other choices are available upon request. This essential supplement can be packaged with any student success text to add value with 'just in time' information for students.

Supplemental Resources

Other Resources

"Infuse student success into any program with our "IDentity" Series booklets!" - Written by national subject matter experts, the material contains strategies and activities for immediate application. Choices include:
- Financial Literacy (Farnoosh Torabi)
- Financial Responsibility (Clearpoint Financial)
- Now You're Thinking about Student Success (Judy Chartrand et.al.)
- Now You're Thinking about Career Success (Judy Chartrand et.al.)
- Ownership (Megan Stone)
- Critical Thinking: A Career Choice (Paul Schuler)
- Identity (Stedman Graham).

"Through partnership opportunities, we offer a variety of assessment options!"
LASSI – The LASSI is a 10-scale, 80-item assessment of students' awareness about and use of learning and study strategies. Addressing skill, will and self-regulation, the focus is on both covert and overt thoughts, behaviors, attitudes and beliefs that relate to successful learning and that can be altered through educational interventions. Available in two formats: Paper ISBN: 0131723154 or Online ISBN: 0131723162 (access card).

"For a truly tailored solution that fosters campus connections and increases retention, talk with us about custom publishing."
Pearson Custom Publishing – We are the largest custom provider for print and media shaped to your course's needs. Please visit us at www.pearsoncustom.com to learn more.

STUDENT SUPPORT – Tools to help make the grade now, and excel in school later.

"Now there's a Smart way for students to save money."
CourseSmart is an exciting new choice for students looking to save money. As an alternative to purchasing the printed textbook, students can purchase an electronic version of the same content. With a CourseSmart eTextbook, students can search the text, make notes online, print out reading assignments that incorporate lecture notes, and bookmark important passages for later review. For more information, or to purchase access to the CourseSmart eTextbook, visit www.coursesmart.com

"Today's students are more inclined than ever to use technology to enhance their learning."
MyStudentSuccessLab will engage students through relevant YouTube videos with 'how to' videos selected 'by students, for students' and help build the skills they need to succeed for ongoing personal and professional development. www.mystudentsuccesslab.com

"Time management is the #1 challenge students face."
Premier Annual Planner - This specially designed, annual 4-color collegiate planner includes an academic planning/resources section, monthly planning section (2 pages/month), weekly planning section (48 weeks; July start date), which facilitate short-term as well as long term planning. Spiral bound, 6x9.

"Journaling activities promote self-discovery and self-awareness."
Student Reflection Journal - Through this vehicle, students are encouraged to track their progress and share their insights, thoughts, and concerns. 8 1/2 x 11. 90 pages.

MyStudentSuccessLab

Start Strong. Finish Stronger.
www.MyStudentSuccessLab.com

MyStudentSuccessLab is an online solution designed to help students acquire the skills they need to succeed for ongoing personal and professional development. They will have access to peer-led video interviews and develop core skills through interactive practice exercises and activities that provide academic, life, and professionalism skills that will transfer to ANY course.

It can accompany any Student Success text or used as a stand-alone course offering.

How will MyStudentSuccessLab make a difference?

Is motivation a challenge, and if so, how do you deal with it?

Video Interviews – Experience peer led video 'by students, for students' of all ages and stages.

How would better class preparation improve the learning experience?

Practice Exercises – Practice skills for each topic - leveled by Bloom's taxonomy.

What could you gain by building critical thinking and problem-solving skills?

Activities – Apply what is being learned to create 'personally relevant' resources through enhanced communication and self-reflection.

PEARSON

MyStudentSuccessLab

Start Strong. Finish Stronger.
www.MyStudentSuccessLab.com

As an instructor, how much easier would it be to assign and assess on MyStudentSuccessLab if you had a Learning Path Diagnostic that reported to the grade book?

Learning Path Diagnostic

- For the **course**, 65 Pre-Course questions (Levels I & II Bloom's) and 65 Post-Course questions (Levels III & IV Bloom's) that link to key learning objectives in each topic.

- For each **topic**, 20 Pre-Test questions (Levels I & II Bloom's) and 20 Post-Test questions (Levels III & IV Bloom's) that link to all learning objectives in the topic.

As a student, how much more engaged would you be if you had access to relevant YouTube videos within MyStudentSuccessLab?

Student Resources

A wealth of resources like our FinishStrong247 YouTube channel with 'just in time' videos selected 'by students, for students'.

MyStudentSuccessLab Topic List -

1. A First Step: Goal Setting
2. Communication
3. Critical Thinking
4. Financial Literacy
5. Information Literacy

6. Learning Preferences
7. Listening and Taking Notes in Class
8. Majors and Careers
9. Memory and Studying
10. Problem Solving

11. Professionalism
12. Reading and Annotating
13. Stress Management
14. Test Taking Skills
15. Time Management

MyStudentSuccessLab Feature set:

Learning Path Diagnostic: 65 Pre-Course (Levels I & II Bloom's) and 65 Post-Course (Levels III & IV Bloom's) / Pre-Test (Levels I & II Bloom's) and Post-Test (Levels III & IV Bloom's).

Topic Overview: Module objectives.

Video Interviews: Real video interviews 'by students, for students' on key issues.

Practice Exercises: Skill-building exercises per topic provide interactive experience and practice.

Activities: Apply what is being learned to create 'personally relevant' resources through enhanced communication and self-reflection.

Student Resources: Pearson Students Facebook page, FinishStrong247 YouTube channel, MySearchLab, Online Dictionary, Plagiarism Guide, Student Planner, and Student Reflection Journal.

Implementation Guide: Grading rubric to support instruction with Overview, Time on Task, Suggested grading, etc.

PEARSON

Pearson Success Tips, 1/e

ISBN-10: 0132788071 • ISBN-13: 9780132788076

Success Tips is a **6-panel laminate** that provides students with information highlights on the most critical topics for student success. These topics include MyStudentSuccessLab, Time Management, Resources All Around You, Now You're Thinking, Maintaining Your Financial Sanity, and Building Your Professional Image. Other choices are available upon request via our www.pearsoncustomlibrary.com program, as well as traditional custom publishing. This essential supplement can packaged with any student success text to add value with 'just in time' information for students.

Features

- **MyStudentSuccessLab** — Helps students 'Start strong, Finish stronger' by getting the most out of this technology with their book.
- **Time Management** — Everyone begins with the same 24 hours in the day, but how well students use their time varies.
- **Resources All Around You** — Builds awareness for the types of resources available on campus for students to take advantage of.
- **Now You're Thinking** — Learning to think critically is imperative to student success.
- **Maintaining Your Financial Sanity** — Paying attention to savings, spending, and borrowing choices is more important than ever.
- **Building Your Professional Image** — Students are motivated by preparing for their future careers through online and in person professionalism tips, self-branding, and image tips.
- **Additional Topics** — Topics above are 'default.' These topics include MyStudentSuccessLab, Time Management, Resources All Around You, Now You're Thinking, Maintaining Your Financial Sanity, and Building Your Professional Image. Other choices are available upon request via our www.pearsoncustomlibrary.com program, as well as traditional custom publishing. This essential supplement can be packaged with any student success text to add value with 'just in time' information for students.

Topic List

- MyStudentSuccessLab*
- Time Management*
- Resources All Around You*
- Now You're Thinking*
- Maintaining Your Financial Sanity*
- Building Your Professional Image*
- Get Ready for Workplace Success
- Civility Paves the Way Toward Success

- Succeeding in Your Diverse World
- Information Literacy is Essential to Success
- Protect Your Personal Data
- Create Your Personal Brand
- Service Learning
- Stay Well and Manage Stress
- Get Things Done with Virtual Teams
- Welcome to Blackboard!

- Welcome to Moodle!
- Welcome to eCollege!
- Set and Achieve Your Goals
- Prepare for Test Success
- Good Notes Are Your Best Study Tool
- Veterans/Military Returning Students

NOTE: those with asterisks are 'default' options; topic selection can be made through Pearson Custom Library at www.pearsoncustomlibrary.com, as well as traditional custom publishing.

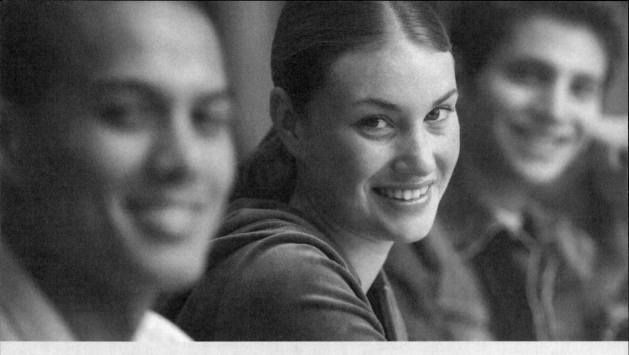

PERSONALIZE THE EXPERIENCE WITH

PEARSON LEARNING SOLUTIONS

FOR STUDENT SUCCESS AND CAREER DEVELOPMENT

The Pearson Custom Library Catalog

With Pearson Custom Library, you can create a custom book by selecting content from our course-specific collections. The collections consist of chapters from Pearson titles like this one, and carefully selected, copyright cleared, third-party content, and pedagogy. The finished product is a print-on-demand custom book that students can purchase in the same way they purchase other course materials.

Custom Media

Pearson Learning Solutions works with you to create a customized technology solution specific to your course requirements and needs. We specialize in a number of best practices including custom websites and portals, animation and simulations, and content conversions and customizations.

Custom Publications

We can develop your original material and create a textbook that meets your course goals. Pearson Learning Solutions works with you on your original manuscript to help refine and strengthen it, ensuring that it meets and exceeds market standards. Pearson Learning Solutions will work with you to select already published content and sequence it to follow your course goals.

Online Education

Pearson Learning Solutions offers customizable online course content for your distance learning classes, hybrid courses, or to enhance the learning experience of your traditional in-classroom students. Courses include a fully developed syllabus, media-rich lecture presentations, audio lectures, a wide variety of assessments, discussion board questions, and a strong instructor resource package.

In the end, the finished product reflects your insight into what your students need to succeed, and puts it into practice. Visit us on the web to learn more at www.pearsoncustom.com/studentsuccess or call 800-777-6872

Introducing CourseSmart, The world's largest online marketplace for digital texts and course materials.

A Smarter Way for Instructors

▶ **CourseSmart saves time.** Instructors can review and compare textbooks and course materials from multiple publishers at one easy-to-navigate, secure website.

▶ **CourseSmart is environmentally sound.** When instructors use CourseSmart, they help reduce the time, cost, and environmental impact of mailing print exam copies.

▶ **CourseSmart reduces student costs.** Instructors can offer students a lower-cost alternative to traditional print textbooks.

▶ **"Add this overview to your syllabus today!"**
REQUIRED COURSE MATERIALS - ALTERNATE VERSION AVAILABLE:

CourseSmart is an exciting new choice for students looking to save money. As an alternative to purchasing the printed textbook, students can purchase an electronic version of the same content. With a CourseSmart eTextbook, students can search the text, make notes online, print out reading assignments that incorporate lecture notes, and bookmark important passages for later review.

A Smarter Way for Students

▶ **CourseSmart is convenient.** Students have instant access to exactly the materials their instructor assigns.

▶ **CourseSmart offers choice.** With CourseSmart, students have a high-quality alternative to the print textbook.

▶ **CourseSmart saves money.** CourseSmart digital solutions can be purchased for up to 50% less than traditional print textbooks.

▶ **CourseSmart offers education value.** Students receive the same content offered in the print textbook enhanced by the search, note-taking, and printing tools of a web application.

CourseSmart is the Smarter Way
To learn for yourself, visit www.coursesmart.com

This is an access-protected site and you will need a password provided to you by a representative from a publishing partner.

C H A P T E R 1

Creating Academic Success

FOCUS QUESTIONS

What are two essential ingredients of a system of study?

Why is each important?

How am I going to apply each?

CHAPTER TERMS

After reading this chapter, define (in your own words) and provide an example for each of the following terms:

- active learning behaviors
- extrinsic reward
- intrinsic reward
- learning modalities
- passive learning behaviors
- Personal Action Statement

Chapter 1	Chapter 2	Chapter 3	Chapter 4	Chapter 5	Chapter 6	Chapter 7	Chapter 8	Chapter 9
Academic Success	Managing Time	Being Productive	Active Listening	Reading Textbooks	Enhancing Memory	Test Preparation	Taking Tests	Continuing Success

A System of Study: The Essential Ingredients

As a college student, you no doubt have experienced—or will experience—approaches toward instruction and requirements for learning that are unlike those experienced in your previous years of education. Recent high school graduates often welcome the greater personal and social freedoms associated with college life. However, along with these freedoms come challenges. No longer does a teacher or a parent oversee your learning; at the postsecondary level, you, the student, are expected to be a self-directed and self-motivated learner.

For the nontraditional student, college life offers a different set of challenges: Returning to school after a hiatus often creates a complicated juggling act among job, family, and academic responsibilities. Whatever the personal circumstances, individual students require their own sets of learning strategies to meet the multifaceted challenges encountered at the college level effectively. This text provides you, the student, with the tools for developing the strategies you need to become a self-directed learner and achieve academic success throughout your college career.

By the time you enter college, you have developed a system of study based on two essential ingredients: your learning behaviors and your learning attitudes. Each is discussed in the following sections.

◑ Your Learning Behaviors

The term *learning behaviors* refers to a variety of actions carried out in an academic situation. These learning behaviors combine to form your system of study. Note that some behaviors are conducive to learning, such as arriving at class several minutes early with notepaper and pen, sitting in the front or middle of a classroom, listening attentively and selectively, asking questions to clarify points, reviewing notes after class, seeking out help when needed, and so on. These are termed **active learning behaviors** because they represent self-responsibility, initiative, and involvement in the learning process. Active learning behaviors lead to successful outcomes—that is, high grades and a smooth path toward graduation.

In contrast, a host of behaviors impede learning, such as skipping classes, sleeping during classes, yielding to distractions, studying after social and leisure activities, and not seeking assistance when needed. These are termed **passive learning behaviors.** Students exhibiting these behaviors do *not* take charge of their learning. Passive learners often are not accustomed to working hard in school; they tend to devote minimal time and effort to their academic life.

This text will introduce you to active learning behaviors at the college level. Each chapter focuses on a group of active learning behaviors—or strategies—related to a major study skills topic. Principal elements of each topic are labeled "Essential Ingredients." Within each chapter you will be given choices of which strategies you will put into practice as you engage in your day-to-day college course work.

Your Learning Attitudes

Your attitude toward all aspects of academic life (going to class, interacting with the instructors, completing assignments, studying) has a huge impact on your accomplishments in college. Successful college students exhibit the following characteristics:

- **Motivation.** They *want* to achieve and are determined to reach their academic goals.
- **Persistence.** They do not let hurdles block personal achievement. When problems arise, they seek out help and persevere until a satisfactory solution is reached.
- **Self-Discipline.** They are willing to make the necessary sacrifices and devote the necessary efforts to receive that college degree. Even more than measures of intelligence, students' levels of self-discipline are associated with academic success.
- **A Personal Support Network.** They have at least one family member or close friend they can rely on for personal encouragement and support. Likewise, they tend to associate with peers who are responsible and caring.

How many of these characteristics do you exhibit at this point in your college career? As you read the upcoming chapters in this text, you will be exploring your outlook toward the many aspects of college life and determining if your attitudes work *for* or *against* your immediate and long-term successes.

ONLINE COURSE WORK

Because distance education can be a very anonymous and independent process, your levels of motivation, persistence, and self-discipline are especially important. Oftentimes students enroll in online courses for reasons that work *against* their success. For example, they are disinterested in the subject, want to get the course out of the way, or think distance education courses are easier than face-to-face instruction. You are much more likely to do well in online course work if you assume the mind-set of "What can I learn?" as opposed to "How little can I do to pass?"

Keep in mind that in college, *you* will be determining your own academic path; thus it is up to you to take responsibility for your successes—or failures. This mission of self-determination and responsibility can be accomplished by an awareness of *why* you are here, *what* you want to accomplish, and *how* you can develop a viewpoint that contributes to personal success.

Critical
Thinking
Task

pause... *and reflect*

- What motivates *you* to achieve?
- Are you persistent when faced with a problem or stumbling block? Provide a personal example.
- Research indicates that self-discipline is more important than IQ in predicting academic success. Why do you think this is? Would you describe yourself as self-disciplined in regard to school? In what areas are you self-disciplined? Describe in what areas you are not self-disciplined, and explain why.
- Who is part of your personal support network?

Learning Modalities

Learning modalities refer to the senses involved in various approaches or strategies for learning and studying. Some strategies favor visual (seeing) modes of learning, while other strategies favor auditory (hearing) or tactile/kinesthetic (feeling/moving) modes, as described below:

- **Visual strategies** help students see information in their mind. Visual methods emphasize organization and spatial images, such as illustrations, charts, maps, and other graphic formats, and often include the use of color and design.
- **Auditory strategies** help students hear information in their mind and often involve listening, verbalizing, and discussing new knowledge. Examples of auditory learning methods are listening to audio files and talking aloud to yourself and others.
- **Tactile/kinesthetic strategies** help students learn through the physical sensations of touching and moving. Examples of tactile/kinesthetic learning methods are the use of real-life models and simulations, videos, role-playing, laboratory work, and field trips.

As a college student, be mindful that:

1. You likely use all three modalities at various times and in varying situations.
2. Generally it is to your advantage to utilize strategies employing multiple modalities, especially when you want to understand and remember content that is new and complex.
3. You will benefit from application and practice strategies, such as use of case studies, examples, demonstrations, and simulations. These types of strategies are most often associated with tactile/kinesthetic modalities.

At the ends of text chapters, you will identify, implement, and evaluate specific visual, auditory, and tactile/kinesthetic learning and study strategies, with the goal of creating a system of study that is successful for *you*.

Critical Thinking Task

pause... *and reflect*

What modalities do you use in a learning situation? For each of the following situations, describe your favored learning strategies. Identify each strategy as using primarily visual, auditory, or tactile/kinesthetic modalities, or a combination of modalities.

- Reading a chapter for a history course.
- Writing the first draft of a research paper.
- Completing math-based homework problems.
- Studying for a test in a science course.

As you transfer suggested learning strategies to your daily course work, you will continually assess the success or failure of the strategies. The following section describes a process to assist you with applying and assessing strategies as you build and strengthen an effective system of study throughout your college career.

A Path to Success: Personal Action Statements

A successful system of study requires much trial and error; you must *try* a strategy to know whether it will work for you. Your academic path in college will be strewn with both successes and failures. Savvy students are alert to which strategies do and do not work for them and, when needed, they take the initiative to substitute other techniques. A **Personal Action Statement** is one way to oversee the piece-by-piece construction of your overall system of study. It is a concise, step-by-step, written plan of one specific strategy—either a behavior or an attitude—that you commit yourself to doing within a predetermined span of time.

Effective Personal Action Statements entail reflection, decision making, and judgment on your part. Because you are required to deliberate, analyze, and critique, each Personal Action Statement is designated as a critical thinking task within the chapters.

Use these guidelines to ensure a successful Personal Action Statement:

Critical
Thinking
Task

- Recognize that a Personal Action Statement is a *commitment to yourself* for action.
- Make the Personal Action Statement manageable by identifying a *specific step* to implement.
- Be realistic and honest with yourself. Identify a step, or strategy, that you *intend* to do, as well as hurdles and rewards for yourself.
- Be willing to put both *thought* and *time* into the Personal Action Statement. Know that, for most students, the results are worth the effort. Soon, you will become adept at identifying and outlining strategies and steps. You will be able to see how the Personal Action Statements can *motivate* you toward action and achievement as you continue to build a system of study for yourself.
- Type your answers for each step. Writing space is limited on text pages. Furthermore, when you type you are able to make more revisions, resulting in higher quality responses.

Here is the setup for the Personal Action Statement:

1. I will: _____.
2. My greatest hurdle to achieving this is: _____.
3. I will eliminate this hurdle by: _____.
4. My time frame for achieving this is:_____.
5. My reward for achieving this is: _____.

On line 1, write what you intend to do. Write a strategy that is specific, realistic, and meaningful to you. Here are some examples:

- "I will study in a library study room three nights next week."
- "I will improve my concentration by taking short breaks every 30 minutes when reading my biology textbook."

Line 2 refers to what you anticipate as being the greatest barrier toward completing the Personal Action Statement. Relying on past experiences and your personal weaknesses, what tends to hinder successful completion of your schoolwork? Examples of hurdles are boredom, the temptation to play an online game, friends dropping by to chat, and your dislike of the subject matter or the instructor. Be honest with yourself: What tends to obstruct your study plans?

On line 3, write *how* you will overcome the hurdle identified in line 2. What can you do realistically to reduce, if not eliminate, this barrier? For instance, you can study with a classmate to relieve boredom, or use an online game only as a break from studying, or be more assertive with your friends, or talk to your professor about your problems.

On line 4, indicate your time frame. When are you going to implement this Personal Action Statement? Make the time frame immediate; begin as soon as possible.

On line 5, identify a reward for completing your Personal Action Statement successfully. It can be an internal or **intrinsic reward** (such as a sense of satisfaction with a high test grade or increased confidence from knowing subject matter) or an external or **extrinsic reward** (such as using a social media site, watching a favorite television program, or talking to a friend).

After completing the Personal Action Statement, place it in an accessible location (such as above your desk, in your planner, or on your computer or smart phone) so that you can refer to it regularly to remind yourself about your intentions.

The last, yet very important, step in this process is the follow-up. At the conclusion of implementing your Personal Action Statement, assess critically what happened. Did you accomplish all that you set out to accomplish? If so, great—reward yourself! Think about the factors that contributed to your success. Use the follow-up as a time to evaluate what happened and anticipate building on your successes.

Also, learn from your partial successes as well as failures. If everything did not work out as anticipated, do not berate yourself. Keep in mind that risk taking is an inherent part of change, and it is inevitable that you will not always be successful when taking risks. However, do learn from your ineffective Personal Action Statements. Analyze what happened. Often students make their Personal Action Statements either too general or too unrealistic (refer to the examples that follow). Think about how you can shape your Personal Action Statement to make it more specific and/or practical.

TOO GENERAL:
I will improve my time management.

MORE SPECIFIC:
I will put class assignments in my planner.

TOO UNREALISTIC:
I will study in the library for three hours *every night* this week.

MORE REALISTIC:
I will study in the library for two hours on three days this week.

How about the anticipated hurdle? Did it actually emerge? If so, were you able to overcome it effectively? Did you discover other impediments? Furthermore, was your time frame appropriate for completing the Personal Action Statement?

Finally, examine your reward. Did you identify a reward that is meaningful to you? Your reward should motivate you to finish a task and make you feel good about succeeding. Dangle a reward in front of yourself that you really want— and can have!

Answering these and similar questions will aid you in analyzing what learning strategies do and do not work for you. It takes deliberate practice to develop effective Personal Action Statements, but the practice is worthwhile. Not only will you be learning about valuable college study strategies, but you also will be learning about yourself!

Conclusion

Your success in college depends on a combination of factors: your behaviors in and out of class, your attitude and commitment to working hard, your awareness of key learning strategies, and your commitment to applying and accessing these strategies in your daily life. The following checklist contains keys to a successful academic year, elements that directly relate to success, satisfaction, and, ultimately, graduation from college. As the year progresses, review the checklist periodically with the goal of accomplishing as much as you can to keep yourself on the track of academic success.

KEYS TO A SUCCESSFUL ACADEMIC YEAR

1. **Be aware of *why* you are attending college, as well as what you expect to get out of college.** Whose decision was it to attend college, yours or your family's? Are you attending the college of your choice? Do you intend to graduate from this or from another college? What do you expect to accomplish in college? Be honest with yourself and clear in your goals.

2. **Know what is *expected of you* in each subject.** Read each syllabus. Make an appointment with each instructor. Attend all classes. Go to review sessions or form your own study group. Ask, and then write down the answers!

3. **Manage your time *wisely*.** Establish a routine; be aware of the dangers of too much free and unstructured time. This is especially true for online course work. Muster the self-discipline to say no to tempting people and activities. Also, create a balance among your academic, personal, and social/leisure lives. Assess your priorities periodically: Do you typically place your academic responsibilities *before* your social aspirations? Do you allow yourself time for fun between the academic and personal demands on your time?

4. **Develop and *use* effective methods of study.** Create a study system that is advantageous to you; choose, use, and evaluate recommended learning strategies. Form beneficial habits early in the year.

5. ***Involve yourself* in college life.** Students who participate in academic, social, and personal campus activities tend to do better academically. Create links between yourself and other people within the college community. Make commitments like these:
   - Join a student organization or club related to your interests or major.
   - Obtain a campus job.
   - Participate in academic support services, such as tutoring, group study sessions, and workshops, or become a tutor or peer educator.
   - Go to campus cultural events, such as guest speakers, fine arts productions, and museum exhibits.
   - Participate in intramural sports and other extracurricular activities.

6. *Avoid* **these hazards:**

- Mishandling of your personal freedom and time
- Misuse of alcohol and drugs
- Mishandling of your personal health
- Mishandling of your best interests

Critical Thinking Task

pause... *and reflect*

Refer to the checklist that offers keys to a successful academic year. At this point in your college career, where would you place yourself?

For each of the six items, write a short paragraph assessing yourself at this time. Include what you have done, as well as what you still need to accomplish.

try it out!

Create a sample Personal Action Statement by choosing one of the items that you still need to accomplish for a successful academic year. Use the following examples as models.

Critical Thinking Task

EXAMPLES OF PERSONAL ACTION STATEMENTS

1. I will: *become more involved in campus life by obtaining an on-campus job.*
2. My greatest hurdle to achieving this is: *not knowing where campus jobs are advertised.*
3. I will eliminate this hurdle by: *(1) asking my adviser about job listings during our meeting on Wednesday, and (2) investigating the Career Services office Web site.*
4. My time frame for completing this is: *by Thursday of this week.*
5. My reward for achieving this is: *the self-satisfaction of knowing that I began looking for a job early in the semester!*

1. I will: *set aside definite times during the afternoon to do both math and chemistry problems.*
2. My greatest hurdle to achieving this is: *the distractions of TV and people in my apartment.*
3. I will eliminate this hurdle by: *studying at a desk at the library during the afternoons when I have large chunks of free time.*
4. My time frame for completing this is: *next Tuesday.*
5. My reward for achieving this is: *not having unfinished work hanging over my head.*

1. I will: *join a campus club related to my interest in an outdoor sport.*
2. My greatest hurdle to achieving this is: *not knowing what clubs are here.*
3. I will eliminate this hurdle by: *checking the Web site for the Office of Student Organizations and narrowing my options to two or three clubs that I will contact and visit.*
4. My time frame for completing this is: *within the next 2 weeks.*
5. My reward for achieving this is: *the knowledge that I actually followed through with something, as well as looking forward to meeting other students.*

Your Personal Action Statement

1. I will: _____

_____

_____

2. My greatest hurdle to achieving this is: _____

_____

_____

3. I will eliminate this hurdle by: _____

_____

_____

4. My time frame for achieving this is: _____

_____

_____

5. My reward for achieving this is: _____

_____

_____

Comprehension Check

eturn to page 1. Without looking back through the chapter, provide a complete answer for each focus question. Then, define each chapter term in your own words and provide an example.

Managing Your Time

FOCUS QUESTIONS

How effectively do I manage my time each day?

Why do college students often have difficulties with managing their time productively?

What are five essential strategies for successful time management?

CHAPTER TERMS

After reading this chapter, define (in your own words) and provide an example for each of the following terms:

- academic planner
- block schedule
- procrastination
- self-regulating attitudes and behaviors

Chapter 1	Chapter 2	Chapter 3	Chapter 4	Chapter 5	Chapter 6	Chapter 7	Chapter 8	Chapter 9
Academic Success	**Managing Time**	Being Productive	Active Listening	Reading Textbooks	Enhancing Memory	Test Preparation	Taking Tests	Continuing Success

Controlling Your Time: Five Essential Ingredients

Many college students face the challenge of how to manage their daily use of time effectively. As a college student, you likely are—or soon will be—juggling a variety of responsibilities and tasks, both personal and academic. The freedom you experience as an undergraduate college student often is unparalleled. For the first time, you are making many daily decisions without having a parent or teacher oversee you. For instance, you decide what time to awaken, whether to eat breakfast, whether to attend class or start an assignment, who to socialize with, and so on. Your decisions, and the subsequent consequences of these decisions, will determine if you are successful in college or not. Read what one freshman wrote; his comments are typical of many first-time college students:

"Time management is my biggest problem. When I have to choose between leisure time and study time, leisure time always wins. I end up cramming the night before a test. One of my roommates, however, starts studying a week ahead of time for his exams and does much better than me. My problem is that nobody is here to make me study. In high school my parents made me study; here at college there always is something else I'd rather be doing." —DEVON

Critical Thinking Task

pause... *and reflect*

Are you similar to Devon when making daily choices and decisions about academics and studying? Answer the following questions:

1. Do you have, or anticipate having, problems choosing study time over leisure time? Describe a situation when you should have studied but did not. Why didn't you study? What did you do instead? How could you have reacted differently? What might help you choose study over leisure?

2. Do you need someone to make you study? If so, who can help you monitor your study time—a roommate, friend, tutor, or relative? Think of ways you can develop the needed self-discipline and structure to focus on academics.

3. Some college students already possess **self-regulating attitudes and behaviors** and are able to monitor their independent time consistently. Self-regulating students have developed the internal discipline, focus, and skills necessary to channel both their time and energies productively. If you fall into this category, describe how you approach your study time. What strategies and attitudes do you adopt to focus on and complete projects, assignments, and other tasks?

4. Interview a present or former student whom you consider skillful about managing his or her time. What strategies does the student use? How did he or she develop those strategies? What suggestions can the student give you about having a productive yet balanced semester? Why would you describe this student as self-regulating?

Each of the following five strategies is essential to the development of a successful system of study. As you read, consider how to incorporate each strategy into your day-to-day activities. Be aware of the importance of these strategies in reducing stress in your daily life:

1. Use a weekly schedule.
2. Use a daily planner.
3. Use a semester calendar.
4. Balance academic with social and personal demands.
5. Avoid procrastination.

USE A WEEKLY SCHEDULE

At the start of each semester you will be faced with many new and unfamiliar situations—different classes, instructors, on-campus or off-campus jobs, and sometimes even changes in your daily living arrangement. With these unfamiliar situations come unaccustomed expectations and responsibilities. Your most immediate need will be a schedule that provides an *overview* of what and where you should be for the week. The weekly schedule will be one tool for you to use to structure your time as you develop sound habits and routines at the beginning of each semester.

Develop a weekly routine that includes these considerations:

1. Class attendance and course work as your main priority.
2. Regular slots for study throughout the week. Look for chunks of time during the day and evening when you are the freshest.
3. For traditional face-to-face courses: Time *before* classes to refresh yourself about the day's topics. Time *after* classes to go over lecture notes, work on assignments, and complete readings.
4. For online courses: Abundant time spread throughout the week to read, review, complete assignments, and seek assistance with questions.

5. Ready access to a study location with minimal distractions.

6. Time to take advantage of campus support services, such as the tutorial center, writing center, counseling center, and career services.

7. Time to attend extracurricular activities, such as fine arts productions, lectures, presentations, student organizations, and community service projects.

8. Time for personal commitments, such as a job, sports, or family responsibilities.

An added personal bonus that results from following these guidelines is that you are associating with others who are responsible, successful, and have similar values and interests. As a result, you will be creating a valuable social network for yourself.

STUDENT VOICES

"Studying earlier in the day helps me concentrate better because I am not tired. Also, I reduce my study time because I am reviewing after class when my recall is the greatest. I concentrate better during short spurts; therefore, I take advantage of the time between classes and small periods throughout the day." —RICARDO

"Using a weekly schedule has greatly reduced my procrastination (my biggest problem). I have begun doing school work during those odd hours that I used to watch TV, visit friends, or play computer games. I am getting *much more* done. This has made a major difference in my week!" —JAMAL

A **block schedule** is an effective format for a weekly schedule because it provides a concise visual representation (Figure 2.1). By filling in the blocks you build a graphic plan for your typical week.

Follow these steps when creating a weekly schedule:

1. First, write in activities that you must do at *fixed times*, such as classes and labs, employment, commuting times, established meetings or appointments, certain family responsibilities, and practice for athletics, band, and so forth. Can you think of other established activities for your typical week?

2. Next, fill in those events for which you can establish your own times to work on and complete. Include three types of activities: academic (assignments, study, tutoring); personal (meals, sleep, household tasks, errands); and social and leisure (calls/emails, exercise, down time).

For *academic* time, take into account these factors:

- Schedule time when you are most alert, using chunks of time that you have available throughout the entire day.

Block format for a weekly schedule.   FIGURE **2.1**

MONDAY	TUESDAY	WEDNESDAY	THURSDAY	FRIDAY	SATURDAY	SUNDAY
7:00	7:00	7:00	7:00	7:00	7:00	7:00
8:00	8:00	8:00	8:00	8:00	8:00	8:00
9:00	9:00	9:00	9:00	9:00	9:00	9:00
10:00	10:00	10:00	10:00	10:00	10:00	10:00
11:00	11:00	11:00	11:00	11:00	11:00	11:00
noon	noon	noon	noon	noon	noon	noon
1:00	1:00	1:00	1:00	1:00	1:00	1:00
2:00	2:00	2:00	2:00	2:00	2:00	2:00
3:00	3:00	3:00	3:00	3:00	3:00	3:00
4:00	4:00	4:00	4:00	4:00	4:00	4:00
5:00	5:00	5:00	5:00	5:00	5:00	5:00
6:00	6:00	6:00	6:00	6:00	6:00	6:00
7:00	7:00	7:00	7:00	7:00	7:00	7:00
8:00	8:00	8:00	8:00	8:00	8:00	8:00
9:00	9:00	9:00	9:00	9:00	9:00	9:00
10:00	10:00	10:00	10:00	10:00	10:00	10:00
11:00	11:00	11:00	11:00	11:00	11:00	11:00
midnight	midnight	midnight	midnight	midnight	midnight	midnight

- Spread out study and review through the week, including weekends.
- Be generous with the amount of time you anticipate needing each week for course work. When you underestimate time needed for academics, you create added complications and stress for yourself. Therefore, allow for substantial study and review time for *each course*. This is especially important for online course work.

ONLINE COURSE WORK

A weekly block schedule is especially important if you are taking one or more online courses. Keep in mind that class time for online courses is a *flexible* event, as opposed to a fixed day and time for face-to-face courses. In addition, many online courses are divided into weekly units, with Friday deadlines for completing the assigned work for the week and/or taking quizzes and tests. As such, here are several recommendations:

- Even though topics and assignments are listed online, complete a separate weekly schedule for yourself. A written hard-copy schedule will help you to organize, clarify, and follow through with online work.
- Consider your online course as "meeting" during a fixed class time during the week, such as either during a Monday/Wednesday slot or a Tuesday/Thursday slot. Fill in these blocks as your standard time to work on the course.
- Fill in additional blocks of time for completing assignments, writing papers, reviewing notes and text material, seeking clarification on weekly content, and preparing for tests.
- Reserve extra time at the end of the week (Thursday/Friday) to ensure that you have ample time to complete work for Friday deadlines.

The bottom line: expect to do *more* advance planning for online courses than for traditional face-to-face courses.

Figure 2.2 shows two students' weekly block schedules. Although each student approached the schedule with differing amounts of information and detail, both evaluated their schedules as effective for them. Note that Student A identified specific times during the week to do work for an online course. Also, note two features of Student B's schedule:

- The darkened blocks represent weekly activities established at fixed times.
- The outlined blocks represent times devoted to academic activities outside of face-to-face class time, including reviewing class notes, studying, and tutoring. Student B actually color-coded these outlined blocks according to subject.

Two examples of weekly block schedules.   FIGURE **2.2**

Student A

MONDAY	TUESDAY	WEDNESDAY	THURSDAY	FRIDAY	SATURDAY	SUNDAY
9:00 class	9:00	9:00 class	9:00	9:00 class	9:00	9:00
10:00 class	10:00 class	10:00 class	10:00 class	10:00 class	10:00	10:00
11:00	11:00 online class	11:00	11:00 online class	11:00	11:00	11:00
noon	noon online class	noon	noon online class	noon	noon	noon
1:00 class	1:00	1:00 class	1:00	1:00 class	1:00	1:00
2:00 work	2:00 lab	2:00 work	2:00	2:00 work	2:00	2:00 work
3:00	3:00	3:00	3:00 study	3:00	3:00	3:00
4:00	4:00	4:00	4:00	4:00	4:00	4:00
5:00	5:00	5:00	5:00	5:00	5:00	5:00
6:00	6:00	6:00	6:00	6:00	6:00	6:00
7:00 study	7:00 S.I. for Bio	7:00	7:00 S.I. for Bio	7:00	7:00	7:00
8:00	8:00 study	8:00 study	8:00 study	8:00	8:00	8:00 study
9:00	9:00	9:00	9:00	9:00	9:00	9:00

(continued)

FIGURE **2.2** *Continued.*

Student B

	MONDAY	TUESDAY	WEDNESDAY	THURSDAY	FRIDAY	SATURDAY	SUNDAY
8:00	8:00	8:00	8:00	8:00	8:00	8:00	8:00
		breakfast		breakfast			
9:00	9:00	9:00	9:00	9:00	9:00	9:00	9:00
	breakfast	review for Chem	breakfast	review for Chem	breakfast		
10:00	10:00	10:00	10:00	10:00	10:00	10:00	10:00
	English class	Chem class	English class	Chem class	English class	workout	
11:00	11:00	11:00	11:00	11:00	11:00	11:00	11:00
		lunch	laundry				
noon	noon	noon	noon	noon	noon	noon	noon
	lunch	Chem lab	lunch	lunch	lunch	begin job	brunch
1:00	1:00	1:00	1:00	1:00	1:00	1:00	1:00
	History class		History class	Writing Center	History class		
2:00	2:00	2:00	2:00	2:00	2:00	2:00	2:00
	Theater class		Theater class		Theater class		pack
3:00	3:00	3:00	3:00	3:00	3:00	3:00	3:00
	review notes	Health class	review notes	Health class	pack		drive school
4:00	4:00	4:00	4:00	4:00	4:00	4:00	4:00
			Big Broth's/Sis		travel home		
5:00	5:00	5:00	5:00	5:00	5:00	5:00	5:00
	workout	dinner	workout	dinner		dinner	dinner
6:00	6:00	6:00	6:00	6:00	6:00	6:00	6:00
	dinner		dinner		dinner	get ready to	
7:00	7:00	7:00	7:00	7:00	7:00	7:00	7:00
	Study Group	review notes	Chem tutoring	read history		go out	English &
8:00	8:00	8:00	8:00	8:00	8:00	8:00	8:00
	for Chem	Econ club	break	TV break	get ready to		history &
9:00	9:00	9:00	9:00	9:00	9:00	9:00	9:00
	TV break		study Health	study theater	go out		theater
10:00	10:00	10:00	10:00	10:00	10:00	10:00	10:00
	study Health	prepare for class	floor meeting	finish English			Homework
11:00	11:00	11:00	11:00	11:00	11:00	11:00	11:00
	SLEEP	SLEEP	SLEEP	SLEEP			SLEEP

itical
inking
ask

pause... *and reflect*

Some students (such as Student B) are more productive when they fill in nearly all of the blocks in their weekly schedule. They favor the structure of prearranged specific daily activities, including meals, sleep, study for *each* subject, and even breaks. Others (such as Student A) find this technique too restrictive and prefer to fill in only those blocks representing the most important activities or the activities that most likely will cause them to procrastinate.

- How about you? Are you more similar to Student A or Student B? Explain.
- Are you more productive when you plan details ahead of time or when you leave blocks open for spontaneous decisions and changes?
- What type of schedule are you more likely to follow and why?
- What types of activities should you be writing down in your weekly schedule?
- How do time management, scheduling, and planning affect *your* levels of stress? Describe a situation in which you created stress for yourself by not managing your time adequately.

STUDENT VOICES

"Last semester I was always rushing to get things done. This semester I am making better judgments about my time. This is reducing the stress in my life. I could not survive without a schedule and would recommend a schedule to every student, especially those students juggling many responsibilities." —NORA

"I highly recommend a weekly schedule to any student taking online classes. I make a spreadsheet for the week and fill in what I have to do. Also, each night I make a list of classes, work, errands, and homework that I need to do the following day. I get such a feeling of accomplishment crossing off the things that I've finished!" —COLIN

try it out!

1. Develop a weekly block schedule for yourself for the current semester (use Figure 2.1). Refer to the two steps described previously:
   - Fill in activities with fixed times.
   - Then fill in activities with flexible times.
2. Refer to the guidelines on pages 13–14. Consider each of the eight items when setting up your schedule.
3. After filling in your weekly block schedule, *use* it. Place it in a location for ready referral. Put a hard copy near your desk or work area, or in your book bag or planner; place an electronic copy in your computer or mobile phone. This weekly schedule will provide you with a framework for establishing your day-to-day routine, so refer to it often, especially at the start of each semester.
4. After a week, **Assess Your Success** by answering these questions:
   - Overall, did the schedule provide you with a needed framework for establishing your daily routine? Explain.
   - Should you have more or fewer activities and details in your schedule?
   - Should you use another format, different design, or color coding for your schedule?
   - Did you refer to your schedule regularly? Why or why not?
   - Will you continue to use a weekly schedule? Why or why not?

Critical
Thinking
Task

USE A DAILY PLANNER

An **academic planner** is a day-to-day log, either in book or electronic format, reminding you of tasks to be accomplished. It is crucial to planning and juggling schoolwork successfully with personal and social activities. A well-used planner is invaluable for keeping you on track with your many and varied plans and responsibilities. Acquire a hard-copy planner that easily fits in your book bag, backpack, or purse. Or, use an electronic planner that is already formatted on your computer or phone. Have your planner accessible so that you can use it daily to add tasks and reminders.

FOR THE DAY

Jot down and prioritize what you plan to do, including:
- *Academic* responsibilities for each course.
- *Personal* commitments or tasks, such as work, shopping, or going to the bank.
- *Social* plans, such as calling someone or a date with friends.

FOR THE WEEK

- Examine each course syllabus for *upcoming* topics, readings, assignments, and test dates.
- Note *extracurricular* activities, such as meetings, athletic obligations, and noncredit classes.
- Be aware of *special commitments*, such as a doctor's appointment, a meeting with your adviser, a tutorial appointment, a theatrical production, or a birthday celebration.

FOR THE SEMESTER

Identify key academic dates, including:

- Deadline for add/drop of courses.
- Deadline for course withdrawal.
- Midterm period.
- Final exam days and times.
- Due dates for long-term course projects or papers.
- Course registration for next term.
- Breaks.

USE A SEMESTER CALENDAR

A calendar provides a long-term overview of your academic year. Use a calendar for a broad view of each semester. When you fill in important semester dates on a calendar, you create a visual picture of upcoming months, although with considerably less detail than your weekly block schedule.

Use a calendar in a similar, although less specific, manner as a planner: As suggested for your planner, chart key academic dates and assignments, projects, and papers as well as special social occasions (such as someone's birthday or a friend's wedding) and personal events (such as the deadline for filing taxes or a vacation). Place the calendar in a visible location for daily reference—a hardcopy calendar over your computer, desk, or work area or on a bulletin board or an electronic calendar in your laptop, netbook, or cell phone. Also, publishers often place calendars within academic planners; note whether your planner provides monthly calendars that are large enough for you to write in and use.

Figure 2.3 reproduces a student's calendar for November.

try it out!

If you don't already have a planner and a calendar, obtain them now!

1. Fill in the planner by referring to the lists (in the previous section) of what to write down "for the day," "for the week," and "for the semester." Check

off each item as you mark the information in your planner. Continue using the planner; have it with you throughout the day.

2. Fill in the calendar with those major events that you want to track throughout the year. Place it in a location for easy reference.

Critical Thinking Task

3. **Assess Your Success:** Did you use your planner daily—that is, did you write or type activities and refer to them consistently? How about your calendar? Did it help you to note major events and due dates? What is the most useful aspect of your time management system thus far? What changes will you make to build a more effective and efficient time management system?

FIGURE **2.3**   *A student's calendar for November.*

SUN	MON	TUES	WED	THURS	FRI	SAT
*register for spring term this week	1	2	3	4	5	6 Melissa is visiting
7 Melissa	8 Math Test Chap. 7–9	9	10	11	12 spring work application due	13 Veterans Day parade
14	15	16	17	18 Intr. Religion Term Paper Due	19 Accounting Test #3	20 Begin break!!
21 →	22 →	23 → Dentist app't. 1:00 pm	24 →	25 → Thanksgiving	26 →	27 →
28 travel to school	29 classes resume	30 Geography Group Presentation				

"I bought a dry-erase board with a monthly calendar and area for notes. I use colored markers to write upcoming due dates on the calendar and create a daily 'To Do' list underneath. This system has been a life saver for me—I am much more organized on a daily and weekly basis." —KYLIE

BALANCE ACADEMIC WITH SOCIAL AND PERSONAL DEMANDS

College students often experience a conflict between their academic requirements and social desires. It is in students' best academic interest to go to sleep before midnight. However, social activities often do not happen until late at night or even in the early morning hours. In residence halls and off-campus complexes, late-night social activities are abundant and appealing. Friends will call or stop by to chat, watch TV, play music or games, accompany you to a party, or ask you to go to an off-campus restaurant or bar. These late-night social activities are tempting and alluring to the college student who wants relief from academic demands, as well as the chance to build a social network and personal sense of belonging.

However, over time, late-night socializing results in students who:

- Become severely sleep deprived.
- Miss classes.
- Are in a dazed, passive mode when they do attend classes.
- Do not put in quality study time during the day (instead, they are sleeping!).
- Have problems organizing, understanding, and remembering subject matter.

All of these listed characteristics contribute to lower academic performances. Thus beware: Late-night socializing and partying can become a potent and dangerous habit!

Some students, however, especially those who are of nontraditional ages, have personal demands that can supersede their academic demands. Time tending to family responsibilities, particularly children, and employment hours can easily push aside academic requirements.

The following strategies can create a balance between your academic and social/personal desires and demands and, as a result, reduce your day-to-day stress levels:

1. *Prioritize.* Make a daily list of tasks according to an order of importance.

2. *Write or type what to accomplish and when to accomplish it,* and then display your list for family and friends to see.

3. *Make others*—friends, family, and employers—*aware of your needs and time constraints* and ask for their *cooperation.*

4. Don't let feelings of guilt guide you in an unproductive direction. Instead, *transform feelings of guilt* into *productive and useful behaviors* related to attaining success in your course work.

5. *Don't overcommit yourself.* Down time is a necessity, not a luxury.

6. *Get adequate sleep.* Research studies demonstrate the drastic and negative effect of inadequate sleep on performance, concentration, and memory. Moreover, a cumulative loss of sleep is associated with increased anxiety, overeating, and illness. Establishing and maintaining a regular weekly schedule helps you get the recommended seven to nine hours of nightly sleep. In addition, you can improve the quality of your nighttime sleep by reducing or eliminating evening consumption of caffeine and alcohol, as well as including some form of physical activity or exercise during the day. Also, consider supplementing nighttime sleep with midday naps of no more than 60 minutes.

7. *Combine academic and social activities.* Find, or create, an environment that provides you with both solid academic activity and enjoyable social connections. Examples are study groups, tutorial or writing center services, campus organizations (such as a biology club or commuter student organization), or other groups that require study hours (such as a fraternity, sorority, or athletic team). For example, Devon (see the nearby "Student Voices") partially solved his time management problems by such a tactic.

"A help to me this semester, believe it or not, is pledging a fraternity. We have study sessions every Monday through Thursday from 6 to 8 p.m. in the library. This helps me, especially because the sessions are mandatory. If I don't go, I get into trouble. I have to hand in all my test grades to the scholastic chairman; if I don't get a 2.0, they won't let me in. This makes me want to do my best and is an added incentive." —DEVON

pause... *and reflect*

1. Do you have problems balancing academic demands with personal responsibilities and/or social events? Explain.
2. When faced with a choice between doing class work and taking care of personal obligations or social desires, what do you usually do? Why?
3. Is it difficult for you to say no to other people's requests, demands, or temptations? Why?
4. Follow these steps:
   - Identify your primary academic obligations for this week.
   - Next, identify your current personal responsibilities.
   - Identify your current social events.
   - Choose one of the seven strategies just described. Explain *how* you will use this strategy to assist you with managing the activities you listed.

AVOID PROCRASTINATION AND REDUCE STRESS

We all are guilty of **procrastination** at various times in our daily lives, be it paying a bill, looking for a job, writing a thank-you note, or doing the laundry. Still, constantly putting off responsibilities and tasks can be a major problem for college students, particularly for the important academic tasks of studying for exams, writing papers, and keeping up with weekly reading assignments.

Procrastination causes undue stress, not to mention poorer performances. Underlying causes of procrastination are often complex and varied. However, having an awareness of *why* you are delaying a task often helps you tackle and complete it. The following list describes some of the common reasons why people procrastinate:

- **Being a perfectionist.** You want to be uncompromisingly perfect at this activity and don't want to do the activity unless you are able to achieve your unrealistically high expectations. Because perfection is essentially impossible to achieve, you continue to postpone the activity.
- **Avoiding failure.** You are concerned that you will fail or perform inadequately and, as a result, will disappoint yourself and others. Therefore, you procrastinate to steer clear of a poor grade—and subsequent failure.
- **Avoiding success.** You are concerned that, as a result of your achievements, you will be expected to handle additional, more difficult, and/or burdensome responsibilities—responsibilities you simply don't want!

- **Being rebellious.** You disagree with *why* you should do an activity, dislike *who* you associate with the activity (such as an assignment from a professor you dislike), or dislike the *task itself* (such as reading text material) and, therefore, put off the activity out of resentfulness or defiance.
- **Feeling overwhelmed.** You consider the task or assignment to be of overbearing proportions and don't know *where* or *how* to begin. Or, you feel overburdened by multiple tasks and decisions and can't seem to get a handle on how to start tackling these activities.
- **Managing time poorly.** You don't plan ahead, use a schedule, or prioritize. You allow less significant tasks or events to get in the way.
- **Being lazy.** You want to avoid the effort and work involved in completing the task.

Critical Thinking Task

pause... *and reflect*

Identify one task, assignment, activity, or decision you should complete within the next week but have been putting off.

Why are you putting off doing this? Use the list of reasons to describe the basis for your procrastination.

The following strategies will help you overcome procrastination:

1. **Know what you should accomplish.** You are more likely to complete a task that you clearly understand. Therefore, know expectations and what you are to undertake. If you are uncertain about what you should accomplish, *ask*!
2. **Determine deadlines.** Have a preset time limit for completing the whole task and, if appropriate, various steps of the task. People tend to follow deadlines established by other people (as opposed to self-imposed deadlines). Therefore, if your instructor does not provide a strict deadline, ask another person—a classmate, roommate, or peer tutor—to establish a reasonable written deadline for you.
3. **Use schedules/planners/calendars.** Write or type *what* you want to do and *when* you will do it. You are more likely to accomplish a task that you write down.
4. **Prioritize.** Assign a level of importance to all tasks. Then categorize activities according to:
   - Will work on today.
   - Will work on today if time.
   - Will save for another day.

5. **Break a task into a series of steps.** Large tasks seem less overwhelming and more approachable if you view them as a series of steps, as opposed to a gigantic whole. At the very least, identify one step that you can do; then do it!

6. **Do the unpleasant task first.** Get the distasteful activity out of the way early, and then work on easier or more desirable activities.

7. **Change how you think about the task.** Instead of thinking of the activity as "dreaded" or "terrible," consider it as a practical means to an end, such as a course that completes a curriculum requirement, a grade to pass a course, or a term paper that gives you research and writing experience.

8. **Have fun with the activity.** See if you can be imaginative with the task, such as adding color and other creative elements to an assignment. Or, you can invent a game or competition for yourself, such as beating a previous time for completing the task or keeping pace with a classmate's score. Sharing and collaborating with other task-minded students can be an enjoyable method for dealing with difficult or disliked subjects.

9. **Establish rewards as personal incentives for completion.**
   - *Extrinsic rewards:* Compensate yourself by watching a TV program or going out to eat at a favorite restaurant.
   - *Intrinsic rewards:* Recognize the personal sense of satisfaction that you receive when you've completed the task. Relish the sense of accomplishment you feel when you are done and can check off the item!

ONLINE COURSE WORK

The likelihood of procrastination increases if you are enrolled in online courses, which lack the built-in structure of weekly face-to-face meetings in a classroom. Furthermore, when isolated at a computer, even routine assignments can seem tedious and time consuming, especially if you are uncomfortable with the technology. As course work piles up, you can easily feel overwhelmed, which leads to increased levels of procrastination. As a result, be especially mindful of monitoring your use of time when enrolled in online courses. These additional strategies will help you:

- Get an overview of course requirements for the whole semester. If the course is not already broken into weekly units, you determine how much course work you can complete realistically each week and mark these units of work in your planner and calendar.
- Be prepared to spend *more* time on online courses than you would on face-to-face courses. On your weekly schedule, block out generous amounts of time to read course materials and complete online assignments.
- Use your planner as a written log of what you intend to complete each day for the online course, and then cross off your daily accomplishments.

Plan ahead when enrolled in online courses. Use weekly schedules and daily planners to help monitor your productivity and maintain your momentum throughout the semester.

try **it out!**

Refer back to the task, assignment, or decision that you have been putting off (p. 26) and the nine strategies to overcome procrastination (pp. 26–27). Identify a strategy you will use to accomplish the task *this week*. Write a paragraph explaining the strategy. Be specific about what and how you will complete the task.

In one week's time, **Assess Your Success:**

Critical Thinking Task

- Did you complete the task? Did the strategy help you complete it? Explain.
- What other strategies will you use to focus your attention and energies on completing an unpleasant activity?

Personal Action Statement: Applying Time Management Techniques

 As described in Chapter 1, a Personal Action Statement is a step-by-step written plan of a specific strategy—in this case a time management strategy—that you are committing yourself to doing. Before developing your own Personal Action Statement, examine the three examples provided and answer these questions:

Critical Thinking Task

1. What are the differences among the plans?
2. Which students created plans that likely will result in successful outcomes? Why?

STUDENT A

1. I will study more for chemistry.
2. My greatest hurdle to achieving this is socializing.
3. I will eliminate this hurdle by socializing less.
4. My time plan for achieving this is soon—before the next test.
5. My reward for achieving this is receiving A grades in the class.

STUDENT B

1. I will study psychology for an hour after lunch each weekday.
2. My greatest hurdle to achieving this is my infatuation with watching reality TV shows.
3. I will eliminate this hurdle by not watching a show until *after* working on psychology for an hour.
4. My time plan for achieving this is to begin on Monday.
5. My reward for achieving this is that I can start catching up with my reading assignments and thus feel better about the class and myself.

STUDENT C

1. I will use a planner to write down due dates for all courses.
2. My greatest hurdle to achieving this is the lack of exact due dates in two of my subjects.
3. I will eliminate this hurdle by penciling in estimations of due dates.
4. My time plan for achieving this is to fill in dates this weekend.
5. My reward for achieving this is a better sense of organization in my daily life.

try it out!

Critical Thinking Task

Learning Modalities, Strategies, and Time Management

Being able to manage your time effectively is a crucial element of a successful system of study. Effective time management involves a combination of strategies and determination on your part. In this section you will identify at least one time management strategy to try out and assess in a week's time.

Your goal is to recognize and refine time management methods that are effective for you.

1. In Figure 2.4, the Time Management Strategies are categorized as predominantly involving visual, auditory, or tactile/kinesthetic modalities. Place a check in the circles next to those strategies that you *do use regularly*. Notice if the strategies you presently use involve mostly one, two, or all three modalities.

2. Next, identify a strategy that you do *not* use consistently but which would likely help you manage your time more effectively and efficiently for the upcoming week. Since it is to your advantage to employ a variety of learning modalities in your system of study, look at a strategy involving a modality different from what you usually use. For instance, if most of your checked circles are in the visual and auditory categories, choose a strategy representing the tactile/kinesthetic modality.

3. Write a Personal Action Statement for that strategy, using the guidelines outlined in Chapter 1:

   - Is your Personal Action Statement a commitment for action?
   - Have you identified specific steps that make your plan manageable?
   - Have you been realistic and honest with yourself? Did you identify a step or strategy that you intend to use, as well as anticipated hurdles and rewards for yourself?
   - Have you put both thought and time into your Personal Action Statement?

4. At week's end, **Assess Your Success.** Refer back to your Personal Action Statement and evaluate your performance by answering the following questions:

   - Did you accomplish what you set out to do? Explain.
   - Were you able to overcome any obstacles? Think about your experience and how successful you were.
   - If you were not satisfied, what additional behaviors or techniques can you implement to make your system of time management effective and efficient for you? Will you try these new strategies in the near future?

Time management strategies and learning modalities.   FIGURE 2.4

TIME MANAGEMENT STRATEGIES	LEARNING MODALITES
○ Set up and use a weekly block schedule to create a "picture" of your week.	
○ Use color to differentiate dates and activities in your schedule, calendar, and/or planner.	
○ In your daily priority list use color and symbols to accentuate activities and steps to complete a project or paper.	**Visual**
○ Create an interest for routine assignments by setting personal goals and rewards and using a fanciful chart to keep track of your progress.	
○ Use sticky notes as daily reminders. Place the notes in visible locations, such as on your computer, bathroom mirror, refrigerator, or front door.	
○ *Other:*	
○ Obtain the schedules for tutorials and group study sessions. Write the days and times in your planner.	
○ Review notes and talk through assignments weekly with a classmate or study buddy.	
○ Schedule time for Web chats.	**Auditory**
○ Request auditory reminders from a roommate or family member. Give yourself daily reminders by talking out loud to yourself.	
○ *Other:*	
○ Create a schedule that varies your activities. Consider ways to modify your approach toward tasks. For example, schedule time to work with others for routine assignments.	
○ Allow extra time for lab work and application activities, especially for difficult subjects.	
○ Schedule study slots for differing places, particularly locations that allow you to move about.	
○ Break up longer assignments into workable steps, writing each step on a note card.	**Tactile/Kinesthetic**
○ Transfer online topics and due dates into a hard-copy schedule.	
○ Post sticky notes with daily reminders. When finished with the task, savor pulling off and discarding the note.	
○ Write a due date earlier than actually needed.	
○ *Other:*	

Your Personal Action Statement

1. I will: _____

    _____

    _____

2. My greatest hurdle to achieving this is: _____

    _____

    _____

3. I will eliminate this hurdle by: _____

    _____

    _____

4. My time frame for achieving this is: _____

    _____

    _____

5. My reward for achieving this is: _____

    _____

    _____

STUDENT VOICES

"I really was not planning on this Personal Action Statement helping me much; however, I have to admit that it worked well. This was the first time I ever made a real schedule for myself, and I've now grown accustomed to using it. With a set schedule, I see the day as a whole and actually get more done, especially in those hidden time areas throughout the day. It's odd to me that something this small can totally change my whole perspective on how, where, and when I spend my time." —CHRIS

Conclusion

Your decisions, and the subsequent consequences of these decisions, will determine how successful you are in college. Calendars, weekly schedules, and daily to-do lists are tools to assist you with the multitude of time management decisions. After all, your time is valuable, so use it wisely!

1. Establish a weekly routine early each semester.
2. Use a planner every day—write or type what to do and when to do it.
3. Put important dates on a calendar to know what events are coming up and avoid being caught off guard.
4. Make wise decisions about balancing your academic responsibilities with social and personal activities.
5. Be aware of when you are procrastinating, and then use strategies that assist you to begin and complete the task.
6. Take charge. Be proactive, and don't allow others to control how you use your time.

Comprehension Check

 eturn to page 11. Without looking back through the chapter, provide a complete answer for each focus question. Then define each chapter term in your own words and provide an example.

Maximizing Your Productivity

FOCUS QUESTIONS

What is the connection between your study location and your work productivity?

Identify your top three distractions. Describe how you can minimize these distractions in order to maximize your concentration.

Describe an ideal study environment for yourself.

CHAPTER TERMS

After reading this chapter, define (in your own words) and provide an example for each of the following terms:

- external distractions
- internal distractions

Chapter 1	Chapter 2	Chapter 3	Chapter 4	Chapter 5	Chapter 6	Chapter 7	Chapter 8	Chapter 9
Academic Success	Managing Time	**Being Productive**	Active Listening	Reading Textbooks	Enhancing Memory	Test Preparation	Taking Tests	Continuing Success

Maximizing Your Productivity: Three Essential Ingredients

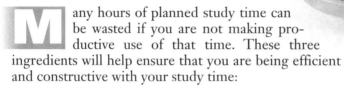

Many hours of planned study time can be wasted if you are not making productive use of that time. These three ingredients will help ensure that you are being efficient and constructive with your study time:

1. Choose a suitable location.
2. Get organized.
3. Minimize distractions.

Choose a Suitable Location

Alongside your planning of *when* you will study should be your planning of *where* to study. You will want to avoid studying in a location that shifts your attention and efforts *away from* what you want to accomplish. Instead, pinpoint a location that is conducive to quality study time and take advantage of this location as much as possible. The following criteria will help you identify a desirable study location:

1. **Is this place *different from* where you sleep, eat, and socialize?** Although convenient, your dormitory room, apartment, or house is often full of distractions. Consider the multitude of distractions surrounding you in such a location—roommates, friends, family members, a comfortable bed, television, personal chores, leisure activities, and so on. You are better off choosing a study place that you associate *only* with academics, such as a spare room, study lounge, empty classroom, tutorial center, or library carrel.

2. **Is this place away from direct foot traffic?** Choose a spot away from others. For example, a living room or a kitchen is often a high-traffic area, whereas other people rarely use an extra room in your house. In the library, an upper floor or corner table usually is better than the busy entranceway and main floor.

3. **Is this place away from loud, distracting noises?** Avoid noisy environments. Research confirms that loud noises interfere with the brain's ability to sort, interpret, and remember information. Thus choose a setting in which you are less likely to encounter distracting sounds emanating from chatty people, music, traffic, television, and the like.

4. **Is this place readily accessible?** (Not accessible for other people who may distract you but accessible for *you*!) Find a location that is available and

easy to get to when you are ready for study. Consider locations nearby—for example, a study lounge in a residence hall or student union, an empty room in a classroom building, an on-campus or off-campus library, or a desk in the basement.

5. **Does this place provide you with the needed flexibility?** Consider your environmental preferences when studying: Do you want space to spread out materials on a long table or floor? Do you prefer soft background noise or complete quiet? Do you like to eat or drink when studying? Do you prefer natural lighting, soft lighting, or bright lighting? Also, do you need a location with an Internet connection? In addition, consider your present lifestyle: Do you need to fit study time around family obligations or an outside job? Personal issues—such as health needs, family demands, employment, home responsibilities, and other commitments—can affect not only when you are able to study but also where you are able to study.

"I have learned *not* to go back to my living space during the day. If I return to my apartment, I get distracted easily and end up doing things other than school work. Instead, I stay on campus and find a location in a campus building to do work. I get a lot more accomplished with this routine." —OLIVIA

"I like to study in a location where I can feed off of the energy of others who are also working, an area that is not too silent yet not too comfortable. My favorite place is a common area in the student union." —MAGGIE

STUDENT VOICES

try it out!

Critical Thinking Task

Rating Your Study Environment

Location A: What specific location do you most often use for study?

Location B: What other location do you also use?

Rate locations A and B by answering the four questions. Use the following point scale:

			Locations
"Yes"	=	2 points	
"Somewhat"	=	1 point	
"No"	=	0 points	A B

1. Is this place different from where you sleep, eat, and socialize? _____ _____
2. Is this place away from direct foot traffic? _____ _____
3. Is this place away from loud noises? _____ _____
4. Is this place readily accessible? _____ _____
5. Does this place provide you with the needed flexibility? _____ _____

Total Points _____ _____

Your total points for each location will be from a low of 0 to a high of 10. The higher your score, the more desirable the location should be for study.

8–10 points: An *excellent* place to concentrate and study. Use it often.

5–7 points: A *fair* study location. Make some changes to lessen distractions.

0–4 points: A *poor* study location. Work on reducing distractions or move to another location.

Write an evaluation of your two locations. Consider these questions:

1. Which location had a higher score, A or B? Why?
2. What are your main distractions at each location?
3. Did your scores surprise you? Do you agree with the ratings?
4. What ways can you reduce distractions at each location?
5. What other locations would be worthwhile for study?

Get Organized: Reduce Stress and Increase Productivity

Organization is a vital component of effective, efficient study. When you organize your environment, you create an important sense of self-control and self-management, reducing your levels of anxiety and stress and increasing your levels of productivity. An active take-charge approach toward arranging your surroundings often mirrors an active can-do approach toward your course work. Also, as you organize yourself and your surroundings, you will be *preparing* to work. You will discover that, when organized, you experience fewer missed appointments, forgotten assignments, lackluster test performances, and other day-to-day hassles and frustrations. As you become more productive, you'll notice a marked decrease in your daily worries and tensions. Following are some suggestions for organizing yourself.

Plan ahead. Keeping track of assignments, due dates, important events, and other short-term and long-term responsibilities is a fundamental aspect of personal planning. Use a paper or electronic schedule—a planner, calendar, and daily to-do list—to prepare and plan in advance.

Have work supplies ready. Anticipate what you will need to complete assignments or activities. Keep your supplies in a central location, such as a desk or bookshelf. If you are a commuter student, keep your supplies in a portable container, such as a plastic storage box or tote bag. Store the container in your car or locker and carry what you need for classes, labs, or assignments.

SUPPLIES FOR COLLEGE STUDENTS

○ Textbooks—hard copies or electronic copies
○ Supplemental CDs, study guides, lab guides, and so forth
○ Notebooks—three-ring binders or spiral bound
○ Computer and printer—your own or in a college computer lab
○ Computer data storage device—USB flash drive or memory card
○ Pens, pencils, and highlighters
○ Paper—plain for printing and lined for notes
○ Index cards
○ Sticky notes
○ Daily planner and semester calendar, either paper or electronic format
○ Stapler, paper clips, scissors, and hole punch
○ Watch (Don't expect classrooms to have accurate clocks, and don't expect that you will be able to check your cell phone or other electronic device for the time.)
○ Alarm clock (can be via a cell phone or computer) to set wake-up alerts and reminders
○ Other: _____

Develop a system of storing materials. Set up a system for organizing and storing course materials. Some students prefer to have separate notebooks, folders, and storage bins for each course. Others use a large binder to organize notes and handouts, by subject, for the semester. Also, create a method for saving and storing computer-based materials (see Online Course Work section). Develop a system that makes sense to you and, importantly, provides an efficient means to access materials as you need them for each course.

Create order for yourself.   An ordered environment will increase your overall work efficiency and productivity. A personal sense of neatness or orderliness differs from individual to individual. Know your preferences and tolerance in regard to cleanliness, room arrangement, and tidiness. Also, recognize that at times you'll be more productive if you rearrange or clean your study location *before* tackling your academic assignments.

ONLINE COURSE WORK

Orderliness is also important for computer, word processing, and Web-based work. Each semester, create virtual folders—labeled for each course—to store your documents, photos, videos, and other course materials. Under each course folder, create sub-folders to further organize your work. Begin by setting up a system that mimics the professor's organization of the course—the course syllabus or outline should help you to create sub-categories according to course topics and a timeline. This is especially true for online courses where course content often is divided into weekly units and assignments. Figure 3.1 illustrates a student's system of folders for an art history course.

Importantly, prepare in advance in case a flash drive is lost or damaged or a computer malfunctions. Be sure to have copies of your work for each course *in more than one location.* Continually back up and copy your work on your personal computer, college network drive, and personal data storage device, such as a USB flash or jump drive.

FIGURE 3.1

try it out!

1. Review the list of college supplies. Mark which ones you already have and which ones you still need to get. Are there other supplies you should have for any of your classes this term? Where are you keeping the supplies so you can easily locate and use them?
2. Do a thorough inspection of your study environment. Characterize the degree of neatness or cleanliness that is important to you and results in your most productive work. Establish your environment accordingly; put supplies in proper receptacles, use shelves or drawers to store items, reduce clutter on your desk or tabletop, and create space to spread out work. Take a photo of the ordered setting; post the photo as a reminder of what your work area *should* look like!

Minimize Distractions and Maximize Concentration

Poor concentration results in inefficient use of your time. Distractions divert concentration, interrupt productive work, and create unwanted stress. Therefore, be conscious of what distracts you and ways to reduce these distractions when doing school work. Distractions fall into two categories:

1. **Internal distractions** originate from within you. Examples are your mind wandering or your lack of motivation.
2. **External distractions** originate from a source outside of you. Examples are the TV, disruptions from family or friends, and loud conversation and noises. To maximize your productivity, consider this advice regarding common external distractions:

   - Study where noise levels are minimal. Research indicates that background noises from conversations, music, or other nearby activities can significantly impede thinking and concentration. Although some people prefer soft music or other low-level sounds when reading and studying, the rule of thumb is to avoid surrounding conversations and extra background noises that will disrupt your concentration.
   - Do not combine study with another activity, such as watching TV, using social media sites, or preparing dinner. Research verifies that doing multiple activities decreases the quality and efficiency of learning. For example, if you study while text messaging friends, you might think you know the information. However, several days later when you need to *use* that information for a test, your accuracy of recall will be reduced because of the seemingly simple activity (text messaging) that interrupted your primary task of studying.

ONLINE COURSE WORK

For the average college student the most powerful distraction is the Internet. When working online, distractions are prevalent because of how readily you can access online games, email, social media and video sites, links to other Web pages, and the like. Research indicates that even the seemingly simple though frequent motions of tapping a touchpad or clicking a mouse create interruptions in our thought processes. Here are several tips to reduce online distractions:

- *Work offline* whenever possible.
- *Turn off all audible sounds* that alert you about an incoming email message, text message, or phone call.
- *Do not open extra hyperlinks and Internet sites*—remember that each click will take you further and further away from your original work material!
- *Work in computer labs.* College labs provide a work-related atmosphere. Plus, lab computers sometimes have specific programs needed for course assignments, as well as common network drives to retrieve and save course materials.
- *Use email, messaging, and nonacademic sites as rewards.* After you have completed a sizeable chunk of work, then you can access email, text messaging, games, social media, and other nonacademic sites (Facebook, Hulu, YouTube, news sites, etc.).

STUDENT VOICES

"I commute to school and have explored suitable locations for study during blocks of time between classes. (The library is too quiet and too warm for me.) Sometimes I use the commuter lounge in the Student Union, especially in the mornings when fewer people are there. However, when I really need to concentrate, I find an unused room in a classroom building. I'm able to spread out my materials, eat my lunch, and move about when necessary." —MELISSA

"I used to study in my dorm room because it was comfortable and convenient, but I found this was not suitable. I got distracted easily and had a tendency to take many breaks. I now study at the library at a remote desk that has no music, no people talking, and nothing else to occupy my time. When I feel bored, I move to another desk in the library." —JOSH *try* it out!

Controlling Distractions

Beside each distraction listed in Figure 3.2, note:

1. Is the distraction *external* or *internal*?
2. How often are you bothered by this distraction: *often*, *sometimes*, or *rarely*?
3. What are ways to *reduce* or *eliminate* this distraction?

Critical
Thinking
Task

pause... *and reflect*

1. Internal distractions tend to be more difficult to eliminate than external distractions. Why?
2. Which type of distractions bothers you most, internal or external? Explain.
3. On the chart in Figure 3.2, check the circles next to your top three distractions. Identify several realistic, practical strategies for reducing each distraction. Ask for suggestions from others.

Rating common distractions.   FIGURE **3.2**

Distractions	E = external I = internal	O = often S = sometimes R = rarely	Ways to Reduce or Eliminate
○ Phone (landline and mobile versions)			
○ Television			
○ Boredom			
○ Computer (including email, social media, games, etc.)			

(continued)

FIGURE **3.2**   *Continued.*

Distractions	E = external I = internal	O = often S = sometimes R = rarely	Ways to Reduce or Eliminate
○ Roommates or family members			
○ Noise or music			
○ Lack of interest			
○ Thinking about other activities or people			
○ People stopping by			
○ Laziness or lack of self-discipline			
○ Disorganization			
○ Worry			
○ Lack of goals for school or career			
○ Sleepiness			
○ Hunger			
○ Other responsibilities			
○ Lack of motivation			
○ *Any others?*			

try it out!

Critical
Thinking
Task

Learning Modalities, Strategies, and Productivity

Productive use of time is a challenge for almost all college students. In this section you will identify at least one strategy to help you to be more efficient with your study time for the upcoming week. The goal is for you to generate a work environment that minimizes distractions and is organized and ready for you to tackle course work.

1. In Figure 3.3, strategies are categorized as predominantly involving visual, auditory, or tactile/kinesthetic modalities. Place checks in the circles next to those strategies that you *do use regularly*. Notice if the strategies you presently use involve mostly one, two, or all three modalities.

2. Identify a strategy that you do *not* use consistently but which would likely help you be more productive *this week*. Generally it is to your advantage to employ a variety of learning modalities in your system of study; therefore, choose a strategy involving a modality that is different from what you usually use.

3. Write a Personal Action Statement for the strategy, using the guidelines outlined in Chapter 1:

   ○ Is your Personal Action Statement a commitment for action?

   ○ Have you identified specific steps that make your plan manageable?

   ○ Have you been realistic and honest with yourself? Did you identify a step or strategy that you intend to do, as well as anticipated hurdles and rewards for yourself?

   ○ Have you put both thought and time into your Personal Action Statement?

4. At week's end, **Assess Your Success.** Refer back to your Personal Action Statement and evaluate your performance by answering the following questions:

   • Did you follow through with what you set out to do? Explain.

   • Were you able to overcome hurdles?

   • Did your reward provide a positive reinforcement for you?

   • If you chose a different study location, are you satisfied with it? Does it seem to fit your particular needs and lifestyle? How prevalent were external and internal distractions? What additional changes do you want to make? Is there a location that might be superior that you will try?

   • If you developed a system for organizing supplies and course materials, are you satisfied with it? Why or why not? What changes do you want to make this upcoming week?

Study location/organizational strategies and learning preferences.

FIGURE 3.3

LOCATION, ORGANIZATION, AND CONCENTRATION STRATEGIES	LEARNING MODALITIES

○ Choose a study location free of noises and other distractions so that you can fully concentrate on visualizing information.

○ Be creative with modifying your favorite study location—change posters, add pictures and colorful decorations, rearrange furniture, and make other novel modifications to make your space visually appealing to you.

○ Create an open, uncluttered study space for yourself.   **Visual**

○ Organize your course materials using color-coded notebooks, folders, and bins.

○ For computer work, organize material in folders according to course and topics.

○ *Other:*

○ Choose a location where you can study out loud with others, such as a lounge or an empty classroom. If by yourself, go to a room where you can close the door and talk out loud to yourself as you study.

○ Go to a tutorial center or homework helper location to discuss your subject matter with others.

○ Obtain CDs or audiotapes that accompany course materials. Record lec-   **Auditory**
tures. (Various computers, phones, and pens have embedded recorders.)
Record yourself as you recite out loud.

○ *Other:*

○ Choose a study location that allows you to move about freely, such as an empty classroom or lab room.

○ Purposely try new and different spaces for study.

○ Be creative with organizing your favorite study location—rearrange furniture to allow movement and get storage bins for course materials.

○ Use interactive Web sites and CDs that accompany course materials.   **Tactile/Kinesthetic**

○ Have index cards of varying sizes, colors, and shapes. Keep the cards organized by subject in storage containers or accordion folders.

○ Obtain supplies so you can rewrite and reorganize notes after class. For each course, have a three-ring binder to hand-write notes. Get a three-hole punch to place course handouts in the binder.

○ *Other:*

Your Personal Action Statement

1. I will: _____

_____

_____

2. My greatest hurdle to achieving this is: _____

_____

_____

3. I will eliminate this hurdle by: _____

_____

_____

4. My time frame for achieving this is: _____

_____

_____

5. My reward for achieving this is: _____

_____

_____

Conclusion

Each week, be mindful of how you can maximize your productivity. Establish a suitable study environment that includes a work space with needed supplies. Also, develop a system of organization for course assignments and computer work. Finally, improve your concentration by minimizing both external and internal distractions.

Comprehension Check

 Return to page 35. Provide a complete answer for each focus question. Then define each chapter term in your own words and provide an example.

Active Listening and Note Taking

FOCUS QUESTIONS

Why is active listening important?

How are active listening and selective listening similar and different?

CHAPTER TERMS

After reading this chapter, define (in your own words) and provide an example for each of the following terms:

- active listening
- listening cues
- nonverbal cues
- selective listening
- verbal cues

Chapter 1	Chapter 2	Chapter 3	Chapter 4	Chapter 5	Chapter 6	Chapter 7	Chapter 8	Chapter 9
Academic Success	Managing Time	Being Productive	**Active Listening**	Reading Textbooks	Enhancing Memory	Test Preparation	Taking Tests	Continuing Success

Active Listening: Three Essential Ingredients

L istening to and hearing information are not the same. You perceive sounds when you *hear* information, whereas *listening* implies more than just a physical act. Listening is an active process—in addition to hearing information, you are *thinking* about the information. Good listening requires alertness and energy; you must pay attention and focus on *what* information is being presented, *why* you should know the information, and *how* you should represent the information in your notes. Therefore, **active listening** involves many decisions on the listener's part. When done well, note taking will help you listen actively.

You will discover that, on a typical exam, the majority of information comes from material covered in class. Therefore, do take notes, even when you have access to content on a PowerPoint presentation or Web site. The purpose of class notes is twofold: To help you *understand* class information, and to help you *remember* class information.

Active listening and note-taking skills are fundamental to college success. The following essential ingredients added before, during, and after each class will maximize your proficiency as a student:

1. Prepare before class.
2. Listen and take notes during class.
3. Follow up after class.

Prepare Before Class

T he most essential strategy is to *go to class*. The importance of class attendance cannot be overstated. Most of the information that will be on tests, as well as directions for assignments and papers, are covered in class. Copying someone else's notes is not the same as personally being in class to observe, listen, and ask questions. Of course, illness and personal emergencies do arise. If you are unable to attend class, let the professor know via an email or phone message. *Before the next class*, find out what was covered in class and any assignments you missed.

Prepare yourself physically for class; resting and eating well will improve your listening concentration. In addition, bring supplies, texts, and completed assignments. If your instructor places notes on a Web site or campus network drive, print out the notes and take them with you to class. Try to arrive a few minutes early to get seated and ready to listen and take notes. You may find the following list of appropriate supplies helpful in preparing for class.

BRING APPROPRIATE SUPPLIES

- **Paper**
    - A *binder with loose-leaf paper* provides you with the most flexibility. Use this type if you print copies of lecture information from a Web site, if you have handouts to insert within your notes, or if your instructor jumps from topic to topic during the lecture. Also, use loose-leaf paper if you prefer to spread out pages for an ordered overview of a topic or time period.
    - A *spiral-bound notebook* tends to be the more convenient type of notebook because the paper is already packaged for you. If your instructor presents information in an orderly, straightforward manner you might favor a spiral-bound notebook, especially one with pockets for handouts.

- **Writing Utensils**
    - *Ink pens* help you write faster and more clearly. Also, your writing will last longer with ink pens rather than with lead pencils.
    - *Lead pencils* generally will make your writing slower and lighter. However, use lead pencils if you do a lot of erasing, such as in a problem-solving mathematics or chemistry course.
    - *Colored markers, pens, and pencils* can be used to provide *emphasis* for key words and phrases.
    - *Digital pens* can store your handwriting or highlighting directly onto your computer. Pens with embedded recorders are useful for recording a lecture while you write. After class, by tapping the end of the pen (which has a sensor) onto the special notepaper, you can play back segments of the lecture that are confusing to you or where your mind wandered and you have gaps in your notes.

Laptop, netbook, or tablet computers are increasingly popular tools for classroom note taking. They can be advantageous if you type faster than you write, and the word processing program can aid you with highlighting important ideas during class time and organizing your notes. Plus, assuming the classroom has a wireless Internet connection, you can access course-related Web sites and PowerPoint materials for in-class discussions and activities. Also, laptops generally have embedded microphones that can be used to record class lectures while taking notes.

But the lure of the Internet also creates a major disadvantage when you use computers during class time. You might easily check email, surf the Web, or watch online videos, all the while insisting that you are paying attention to the class lecture. Research confirms that this type of multitasking *does* affect concentration. Although you might be very accustomed to juggling a number of technological tasks, in the learning environment of a classroom active listening is best accomplished when your attention and thoughts are directed only toward class topics.

BE FAMILIAR WITH THE MATERIAL

- **Read, or at least skim through, text assignments or online information** to provide background and better understanding of ideas to be presented in the lecture. Consider keeping your text open during class for easy referral when (1) the instructor's lecture parallels the text information, (2) the instructor mentions the text frequently, or (3) the text presents the subject matter in a clear, easily understood format.
- **Look over notes from the previous lecture** to refresh your memory about where the lecture ended and what topics were covered. This refresher provides a transition between class sessions and helps focus your attention on the current day's topic.
- **Look over written or online assignments** that the instructor likely will refer to during class.

Critical Thinking Task

pause... *and reflect*

1. What should you do *before* class for each course you are enrolled in this term? Using Figure 4.1, fill in the chart indicating your preparation for each subject.
2. A universal recommendation is for students to choose a seat in the front of each classroom. When sitting in the front, you will be able to hear and see better. Name two other reasons why you should choose a seat in the front of a classroom.

"Two years ago I had one exceptionally bad semester where I did nothing at all (which included skipping most classes, some tests, and two finals). Afterward, I was on academic probation and then dismissed from college. I worked for two years. Now I'm trying college again with a different attitude. One thing that has influenced my performance is that I figured out what each class hour costs me. I added tuition, books, meals, housing, and all fees and divided the total by the number of class hours in a semester (256 for me). This semester, each class I miss costs me about $33! I figure since the class is paid for, I'll go and get my $33 worth!" —MIKE

Preparation by subject.   FIGURE **4.1**

Subject	Supplies needed for class	Type of preparation for class

Listen and Take Notes During Class

reating notes is a major component of active listening and involvement during class. Note taking helps you be more alert, discriminate important points, and organize information, all of which are keys to understanding and remembering. Note taking is important not only during lectures but also when listening to course-related movies, videos, and online DVDs. Take into account the following five factors as you listen and take notes.

1. LISTEN SELECTIVELY

Focus on *ideas*, not just words. Throughout the lecture, continually ask yourself, "What are the important points that the instructor is trying to get across?" Then write down enough information to help you understand those points. **Selective listening** involves an awareness of what is and is not important enough to write down. Thus selective listening requires active decision making on your part. Instead of writing down everything the instructor says, choose main ideas and corresponding supporting points, including explanations and examples. As you listen, ask yourself questions that will help you to pick out noteworthy ideas:

Critical
Thinking
Task

- "What is the *topic*?"
- "What do I need *to know* about the topic?"
- "Why is this topic *important*?"

- "What is an *example* of the topic?"
- "How did this event or procedure *come about*?"

If you are unsure of how much information to write down in your notes, it is best to err on the side of putting down *too much* rather than *too little*. When you review notes after class, you will have the opportunity to highlight key points while eliminating redundant information.

During lectures, instructors give many clues as to what is and is not important, termed **listening cues.** Keep in mind: If your instructor thinks an idea is important, that idea likely will be on an upcoming test; thus you want to capture the idea and related information in your notes.

Verbal cues are what your instructor *says* that signals an idea is important enough to write down. For example, your instructor *repeats information* (making sure you hear and write it down), *pauses or slows down* when talking (giving you time to write down information), or *talks louder* (ensuring that you hear).

Nonverbal cues are what your instructor *does* that indicates an idea is important. For example, your instructor *uses hand gestures* (to help explain important information), *points to words on the board* (to make sure you see and write the information), or walks among students *looking at their notes* (to see if they are writing down correct information).

Critical
Thinking
Task

pause.... *and reflect*

What verbal and nonverbal cues do your instructors use to signal important ideas? Target a course in which you will be listening to lectures for the upcoming week. During class, be attentive to your instructor's cues. Keep a diary of your observations for the week.

Verbal cues:

_____

_____

Nonverbal cues:

_____

_____

2. TAKE CONCISE NOTES

In many classes, you will be quickly writing or typing numerous ideas; therefore, use as few words as you need to communicate these ideas. Here are some tips to help you be concise and succinct.

Use phrases, not whole sentences. Focus on those words that convey *ideas* within statements. What words are necessary to write down to communicate these ideas? You can usually eliminate adjectives, adverbs, prepositions, and conjunctions and still get across the core meaning. Therefore, in your note taking, focus on the *subject* or *topic* and *what you need to know* about the topic, as illustrated here:

> *Instructor says*, "Both external and internal distractions contribute to inadequate attention spans of college students attending large introductory-level lecture classes."
>
> *You write*, "external & internal distract's ⟶ poor attention of students in lecture classes"
>
> *After class*: You go over what you wrote and BOX the terms "external and internal distractions" for *emphasis* and add *examples* for *clarity*.

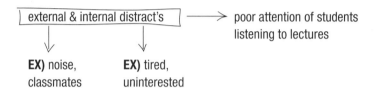

Use abbreviations and symbols. Accustom yourself to using abbreviations and symbols when taking notes. Both will help you reduce the quantity of writing necessary to get ideas across on paper. Repeat abbreviations and symbols within your notes so they become familiar and identifiable to you. Here are some techniques for shortening words:

- Use beginning letters of words or phrases:
    "without" = w/o
    "overdose" = OD
    "sign on" = S.O.
    "as soon as possible" = asap
- Use beginning syllables:
    "anthropology" = anthro
    "demonstration" = demo
    "approximately" = approx
- Remove vowels because the tendency is to recognize words by consonants:
    "explosion" = explsn
    "check" = chck
    "notebook" = notebk
- Use the beginning and end of words:
    "abbreviations" = abbrev's
    "continued" = cont'd
    "additional" = add'l

- Use common characters and symbols:
    - ? = "I don't understand"
    - @ = "at"
    - ⟶ = "linked to or causes"
    - * or ! = "important"
- Use mathematical signs:
    - >< represent "greater than/less than"
    - = means "equal to"
    - # for "number"
    - ~ means "approximately"
    - + for "and"

try **it out!**

Critical Thinking Task

Practice your note-taking skills: Imagine you are listening to the following passage in a class. Create your class notes on a separate sheet of paper. Be *selective* (focus on important ideas), and be *concise* (use phrases and abbreviations and symbols).

Consider the difference between "hearing" and "listening." Hearing is simply the physical function of perceiving sound, whereas listening involves thoughtful attention to those sounds as received by an individual. There are three types of listening: casual, attentive, and evaluative. Casual listening is when one listens to understand but not necessarily to remember. Examples include listening to a friend talk or to the radio or TV. Most of everyday listening is classified as casual listening. On the other hand, a high degree of remembering is a distinctive characteristic of attentive listening, which involves more thought, alertness, and energy than does casual listening. Most of college students' classroom listening should be of this type. Bear in mind that note taking helps an individual to listen attentively. The type of listening requiring the most thought process and energy is evaluative listening. For this category, not only does the listener want to remember, but he also intends to assess information heard. For instance, in a literature course, the instructor gives an assignment to attend a poetry reading and write a critique of a recited poem. The student would be listening to the poem with the intent of assessing critically—thus evaluative listening. Taking notes strengthens one's evaluative listening skills.

Afterward, compare your notes with the sample notes in Figure 4.2.

3. BE CLEAR

Make your notes understandable enough for *you*. After class, you will review the day's lesson; at this point, you will be able to clarify ideas further by rewriting information, adding explanations and examples, and integrating text material.

Thus, be generous with paper as you take class notes. Avoid cramming topics together on the pages. Instead, leave ample spaces between ideas, especially when you know that information is missing. Consider writing on one side of the paper only so that you will have the back to add information, if needed.

In addition, standardize a method for organizing your notes. Always place the subject, date, and topic at the start of the day's notes. As you write, consider the arrangement of ideas. Write main ideas at the left margin and then indent supporting ideas and details. Underline or capitalize headings. Use numbers or letters to itemize separate points. Where appropriate, categorize ideas and add formulas and other visual aids. Include examples from class, and allow space to add more examples and explanations later. Figure 4.2 exemplifies concise, clear, well-organized notes.

Sample class notes.   FIGURE **4.2**

Learning Strategies — Oct. 9   Subject, date, and
                                                       topic at top of page.

HEARING vs. LISTENING (cont'd)

I.   Difference between:
          ** Important ——→ know **   Visual emphasis.

     A.   Hear'g – physical act of perceiv'g sound   Use of abbreviations
     B.   Listen'g – involves thought & attention   and symbols.

II. 3 types Listen'g: Topic in headings with
                                                       supporting details itemized
     A.   Casual   –need to understand, not remember beneath.
                    (used most often)
                    ex.→ talk w/ friend

     B.   Attentive –high am't. remembering, ↑ thought Illustrations and
                    (notetakg helps)   examples.
                    ex.→ in lecture class

                                                       Spaces between topics.
                                                       Extra space to add infor-
                                                       mation after class.

     C.   Evaluative –most thought & energy b/c assessing
                    (note taking helps)

     * see chapter 4 in text   References to text.

4. BE ACCURATE

To ensure that you are representing the ideas accurately within your notes, do the following:

- **Examine your notes *soon* after class.** Go back over your notes while the information from the class is still fresh in your mind, usually within 24 hours after the class.
- **Consult your textbook, lab manual, or other reference source.** If you notice a discrepancy between your class notes and the text or other written source, seek clarification from your instructor, graduate assistant, or tutor.
- **Go over class information with peers.** One of the most effective means for review of class notes is regular attendance at peer-led study groups. If you are unable to locate formal study/review groups, establish your own by inviting classmates (who are serious, capable students) to join you weekly for collaborative review.

ONLINE COURSE WORK

If your instructor posts lecture notes online or on a campus common network, bring them with you to class—either the downloaded hard copies or copies on your laptop computer. It is important that you *use* these notes during class. Adding and clarifying information will keep you engaged in the lecture and help you understand and remember what occurred during the class session. Be alert to your instructor's emphasis of key points using verbal and nonverbal cues, then insert information and examples that help explain ideas. Circle or highlight key terms and phrases; use your system of abbreviations and symbols to illuminate important material. Also, your handwriting and highlighting help to differentiate your additions from the instructor's content. Through this activity in class you are beginning to create a study guide for yourself, as detailed in the following section. (After class, you still will need to review your notes and continue with your study guide; see Figures 4.3 and 4.4.)

---

5. PAY ATTENTION

Paying attention is a key element of effective listening and note taking. Daydreaming is a problem for many students. Physically being in class is ineffectual if you are not also mentally attending to class.

The foremost tactic for maintaining your concentration is willfully wanting to pay attention. In the nearby "Student Voices," notice Bernice's choice of the word *intend* when describing how she improved her alertness in her course.

Personal determination plays a huge role in attentiveness and concentration, even in boring or undesirable situations.

Participate in class. *Answer* questions. *Comment* on topics. *Ask* for clarification. Your involvement and participation can enliven a lecture and keep you alert.

Study guide with text references and summary.   FIGURE 4.3

BIOLOGY   4/11
                    class notes – Chap. 15, Carboxylic Acids

Carboxylic Acids contain the carboxyl grp.
        O   – a hydroxyl grp. Bonded to carbonyl C
        ||
R – C – OH – Is polar, meaning it will form H+ bonds causing high
              melting/boiling pts.

Names: / see CHART in CHAP 15 /
1) Methanoic acid – ant & bee stings
2) Ethanoic acid – vinegar ————————→   / Will hydrogen bond cause
3) Propanoic acid – dairy products   high melt'g/boil'g pts? /
4) Butanoic acid – rancid butter
5) Oxalic acid – rhubarb
6) Citric acid – sour taste in lemon
7) Lactic acid – sour milk

Naming C.A.'s   / full rules on p. 437 /
* oic ending
* the C on carboxylic acid is #1
* for anions, change to "–ate" ending & omit "acid"

DIMER – special H+ bonding structure CA's may take on.

   / Note structure on p. 438 **GOOD TEST QUESTION** /

SUMMARY:
Carboxylic Acids contain the carboxyl group. They are long, straight changes
called fatty acids from hydrolysis of dietary fats. There are seven types, named
according to rules of oic, C on carboxylic acid & changing –ate to acid. A
dimer is a special H+ structure.

STUDY GUIDE created AFTER class
The following are after-class additions:

1. Numbers to organize listing

2. Additions from related text chapter

3. A written summary of key points   [Notes contributed by Adrienne Runk]

FIGURE **4.4**   *Study guide for Web-based notes.*

Web Notes		INTRODUCTION to GEOLOGY CHARACTERISTICS OF SEDIMENTARY ROCKS			Week Two
Type of Rock	Sediment	Environment	Mineral	Chemical Composition	OTHER INFO 1. carbonate sand & mud
LIMESTONE	Calcite Shells (alike) ↓↑	Shallow warm oceans	Calcite (alike) ↓↑	CaCO3 (alike) ↓↑	2. has to be shallow & warm b/c organisms making the shells don't live in cold water 3. calcite dissolves in cold water
CHALK	Microscopic Calcite Shells	Quiet deep sea floor; organisms fall to the bottom when they die	Calcite	CaCO3	**SIMILAR to Limestone
CHERT	Tiny Silica Shells	↓↑ (alike) Quiet deep sea floor; colder water	Opal Quartz	SiO2	Siliceous Sediment ↓↑ (vs.)
EVAPORITES	Gypsum Halite	Dried lakes or oceans	Bypsum Halite Anhydrite	Gypsum-CaCO3 Halite-NaC1	1. Evaporite Sediment 2. made in desert climates—Death Valley, Persian Gulf
PEAT/COAL	Plant Debris	Swamp Bog	Coal Oil Gas	Carbon	1. pure organic matter 2. Function: preserves organic matter by keeping animals out that would eat it

Study Questions:
1. What are the 5 types of sedimentary rock?
2. Describe the composition, environment, and key features of each.
3. Which types are similar?

During class the student:
1. Added last column ("OTHER INFO") to write additional information.
2. Added phrases linking certain types: "↓↑(alike)".
3. Highlighted the names of rocks and other terms.

After class the student:
4. Wrote three study questions on the back of the paper.

"I intended to pay closer attention in accounting class. I did have my moments of daydreaming, but, for the most part, I did listen and followed along with the material being presented. I actually knew how to do homework problems; it was a nice feeling!" —BERNICE

ONLINE COURSE WORK

The anonymous nature of an online course makes active participation especially important. Know when your instructor is available online so you can initiate emails and ask for feedback and clarification throughout the course. Also, be sure to participate regularly in electronic discussion boards and chat rooms for the course.

Sit up front. Being able to see and hear better should help you to pay attention. Also, knowing you are highly visible to your instructor can motivate you to be more alert and involved in class.

Create physical movement. Bring a caffeinated drink (if permitted). Chewing on gum or candy can help keep your mind activated. Switch colored pens. Applying gentle pressure to stimulation points on your body (top of your head, sides of the back of your neck, or back of your hand between your thumb and forefinger) can aid in keeping you alert. Even slight movements, such as wiggling your leg, can help you stay awake and focused.

"There is no substitute for taking your own notes. Note taking helps me pay attention to a lecture as well as organize and remember the ideas. As every student quickly learns, merely sitting through a class is not enough to ensure good grades." —SURI

"Unlike in the past, I now look over my notes more frequently and actually read the text as assigned. Now I feel *much more* comfortable during class discussions since I am more familiar with the material, instead of hearing it for the first time right there in class." —JUSTIN

Follow Up After Class

Review your class notes and create a study guide for yourself. To reduce the progression of forgetting, incorporate this step within 24 hours after a class. By immediately reviewing, you will be checking your understanding of class material. Do the following as you go over your notes:

- Highlight key words or phrases.
- Condense information.
- Fill in incomplete material.
- Add explanations and examples in your own words.
- Refer to text material.
- Summarize key points.
- Think about what you need to know for the upcoming quiz, exam, or discussion, and develop questions for yourself.

By adding, condensing, emphasizing, and organizing lecture information, you will be creating a valuable study guide for yourself. Figures 4.3 and 4.4 illustrate differing study guides. By reviewing and *doing something* with notes soon after class, you are immediately integrating study with note taking. That is, you are learning the subject matter while it is still fresh in your mind. This strategy is considerably more effective and efficient than the usual method of only reviewing class notes days—or even hours—before the exam. Because reviewing notes and creating a study guide *soon after class* is pivotal for understanding and remembering class information, incorporate this study strategy into your weekly routine from the beginning of the semester.

Review weekly. For an overview of the subject matter, each week skim through the study guides you created from your class notes. This will help you see connections among topics. Reinforce these connections by saying key ideas out loud.

Use academic support services. Participate in group study and review sessions regularly. If you don't understand something, ask your instructor, graduate student, or tutor for an explanation.

Use the Cornell note-taking system. A popular method of note taking is the Cornell system (Pauk, 2001, pp. 236–241). A key component of this system is the wide formal columns on each sheet of notepaper used for after-class study guides and review:

- A 2½-inch cue column on the left side of the paper to develop questions
- A 2-inch strip at the bottom of the paper to write a summary

The steps for the Cornell note-taking system are as follows:

1. During class, take notes using the 6-inch space on the right side of the note-paper.
2. Soon after class, go back over your notes, filling in information.
3. Use the cue column to develop questions based on each key idea.
4. Cover the body of your notes (in the 6-inch area) with a sheet of paper. Recite the answer to each question in the cue column, checking your answer by uncovering the body of your notes. Repeat this step until your answers are correct.
5. Use the 2-inch space at the bottom to write a concise summary of ideas on the page.
6. Review your notes right away to reinforce the material.
7. Reflect about the importance of the overall ideas.

Figure 4.5 illustrates the Cornell system of note taking.

ONLINE COURSE WORK

As suggested in Chapter 2, in an online course structure your week by creating regular "class" times to read and work on content, as well as additional "study" times to complete assignments. As with face-to-face courses, review course content *throughout the week*.

try it out!

Critical Thinking Task

Target a course in which you take many and frequent class notes. Within 24 hours after each class for the next week, review your notes and create a study guide using the strategies illustrated in Figures 4.2, 4.3, 4.4, and 4.5.

Dealing with Difficult Lecturers

igure 4.6 summarizes common difficulties that students encounter in lectures, as well as suggestions for dealing with the difficulties and adapting to instructors' styles. What information can you add?

FIGURE **4.5**   *Cornell system of note taking.*

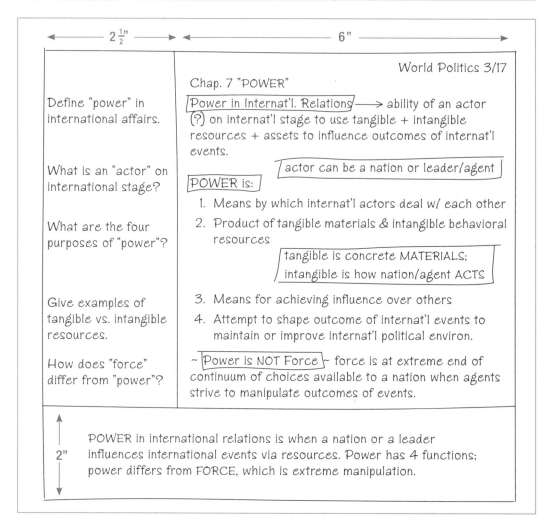

<table>
<tr><td colspan="2" align="right">World Politics 3/17</td></tr>
</table>

2 ½″	6″
	World Politics 3/17
	Chap. 7 "POWER"
Define "power" in international affairs.	Power in Internat'l. Relations ⟶ ability of an actor (?) on internat'l stage to use tangible + intangible resources + assets to influence outcomes of internat'l events.
What is an "actor" on international stage?	actor can be a nation or leader/agent
	POWER is:
	1. Means by which internat'l actors deal w/ each other
What are the four purposes of "power"?	2. Product of tangible materials & intangible behavioral resources
	tangible is concrete MATERIALS; intangible is how nation/agent ACTS
Give examples of tangible vs. intangible resources.	3. Means for achieving influence over others
	4. Attempt to shape outcome of internat'l events to maintain or improve internat'l political environ.
How does "force" differ from "power"?	~ Power is NOT Force ⟩ force is at extreme end of continuum of choices available to a nation when agents strive to manipulate outcomes of events.
2″	POWER in international relations is when a nation or a leader influences international events via resources. Power has 4 functions; power differs from FORCE, which is extreme manipulation.

[The after-class additions are ⟦boxed⟧ in the above notes.]
1. *During class,* the student took notes on the six-inch right side of paper.
2. *Soon afterward,* the student went back over notes: clarified terms (*actor, tangible, intangible*) and underlined/highlighted to emphasize key concepts/terms;
3. Created five questions in the "cue column";
4. Covered the notes and recited answers to each question;
5. Wrote a summary in the bottom 2-inch space;
6. Reviewed immediately; and then
7. Reflected on the material's overall importance.

Dealing with difficult lecturers.

FIGURE **4.6**

Instructor Characteristics	Suggestions for Students
Talks over students' heads; uses complex words and ideas.	○ Review chapter to be covered. ○ Ask lots of questions. ○ Talk with the instructor out of class to seek explanations.
Jumps from topic to topic; unorganized.	○ Reorganize notes *after* each class. ○ Have a three-ring binder with the aim of using a separate sheet of paper for each topic; reorganize the pages after class. ○ Leave space within the notes or use the back of the notepaper to reorganize notes and fill in details after class. ○ Record (with permission), and use the recording to help you reorganize notes, by topic, after class. ○ Read and review the textbook before and after class to give you background information about organization of topics. ○ Ask lots of questions in and out of class.
Talks too fast.	○ Review notes after every class—use the text and other readings to fill in what you missed. ○ Record (with permission) and listen after class and fill in parts you missed. ○ Jot down *only* key points and ideas—leave spaces to fill in added details after class. ○ See the instructor during office hours to review what you missed or don't fully understand. ○ Review notes regularly with other students. ○ Ask the instructor to slow down and/or to repeat information.
Talks with a foreign accent.	○ Sit in the front of the room near the instructor. ○ Talk to the instructor one on one; this will help you get used to the instructor's manner of speech. ○ Ask the instructor to repeat information. ○ Listen carefully and ask for visual reinforcements, such as the use of projectors, the board, and handouts. ○ Review notes regularly with other students.

(continued)

FIGURE **4.6** *Continued.*

Instructor Characteristics	Suggestions for Students
Presents information in a life-less, boring manner.	○ Sit near the instructor. ○ Bring colorful supplies—at least create lively notes for yourself! ○ Ask questions and urge classmates to ask questions to enliven presentation.
Is condescending or impersonal toward students.	○ See if you can talk to and form a relationship with the instructor. ○ Ignore it. ○ Seek help and personal affirmation out of class.
Skips over important topics that likely will be on tests.	○ Bring up those topics; ask questions. ○ Ask the instructor to review major topics on the test. ○ Go to peer-led study/review or tutorial sessions.
Gives a large amount of information.	○ Dissect information when reviewing notes after class. ○ Go over information in study groups.
Repeats topics too much, or students are too familiar with topics.	○ Ask questions to possibly move the instructor ahead. ○ Ask about related topics. ○ Use markers or colored pens while in class to reinforce and emphasize major concepts within your notes. ○ Look ahead to future topics.
Doesn't want to be bothered explaining material.	○ Be persistent; keep asking questions. ○ Personally talk to the instructor after class—try to establish a working relationship. ○ Seek help from a tutor or another student.
Is unprepared for class or online instruction.	○ Go to tutoring to fill in gaps. ○ Read and study the textbook before and after class. ○ Ask lots of questions and show interest; this might spur the instructor to better prepare for class.
Doesn't respond to emails or give feedback about online assignments.	○ Find out the instructor's office hours. Call during that time or make a face-to-face appointment. ○ Leave a clear message on the instructor's answering machine or with the office secretary.

Others:

and reflect

Consider the instructors for your classes. Which instructors have exhibited characteristics that you found to be difficult to listen to or distracting? Use Figure 4.6 to identify your instructors' characteristics and accompanying suggestions.

- Which suggestions will you use for that class?
- What additional suggestions can you add?

Use Figure 4.7 to keep track of suggestions and adaptations for the classes you have identified.

try it out!

Learning Modalities, Strategies, and Active Listening/Note Taking

By combining knowledge, time, and practice, you are developing a system of listening and note taking that is most effective for you. Assess your strategies regularly: Do you need to improve class preparation? Do you want to modify how you listen or where you sit in a particular class? Should you be trying a different format for note taking? The following steps will help you to fine-tune your approaches toward listening and note taking.

1. In Figure 4.8, Listening and Note-Taking Strategies are categorized as predominantly involving visual, auditory, or tactile/kinesthetic modalities. Place checks in the circles next to those strategies that you *do use regularly*.
2. Next, identify a strategy that you do *not* use consistently but that would likely help during the upcoming week. Since it is to your advantage to employ a variety of learning modalities in your system of study, look at a strategy involving a modality different from what you usually use. Refer to the examples in Figure 4.9 for suggestions.
3. Write a Personal Action Statement for that strategy.
4. At the end of the week, **Assess Your Success:**
   - Did you follow through and reward yourself accordingly? Explain.
   - Did the hurdle materialize, and did you manage it effectively?
   - Examine your habits before, during, and after a class. Describe the changes you need to make.

FIGURE **4.7**   *Chart for tracking suggestions.*

INSTRUCTOR/SUBJECT	STRATEGIES

Active listening strategies and learning modalities.

FIGURE 4.8

LISTENING AND NOTE-TAKING STRATEGIES	LEARNING MODALITIES
○ Before class, skim through the chapter and read the summary. This will assist you to see the whole picture of the lecture topic.	
○ During class, sit up front so that you can readily see the board, screens, overhead transparencies, and other visual presentations.	
○ Form a mental "picture" of ideas being presented during a lecture. Write down associations, relationships, and illustrations in your notes.	
○ Use three-ring binders. Write on one side so that you can spread out the sheets of paper when studying. Leave generous space between ideas in your notes. Have at least two colors of pens for use during class note taking.	
○ Prepare a written weekly log of when you will review notes (soon after class) and complete course assignments.	**Visual**
○ After class, add visual emphasis by highlighting and color-coding key concepts, terms, and phrases within your notes. Use differing fonts for typed notes.	
○ Reduce your class notes by creating visual summaries, such as charts, graphs, and timelines, that show the organization of information and relationships among ideas.	
○ While reviewing lecture notes, picture how the information fits into the text and other readings.	
○ *Other:*	
○ Participate in class; ask and answer questions. For online course work, participate in discussion groups.	
○ Tape the lecture. Use a high-quality recorder, computer, or specialized pen with an embedded microphone. After class, use the recording to review areas of the lecture that you are unsure about.	
○ Leave spaces when taking notes so that you can fill in missing information when you review later.	
○ After class, expand your notes by referring to the textbook, listening to an audio recording, or talking with classmates.	**Auditory**
○ When reviewing your lecture notes, recite out loud to yourself. Record yourself and listen while in your car or use your MP3 player.	
○ Participate in group review sessions. Compare and discuss notes with others.	
○ Teach others; this will clarify information and reinforce what you know.	
○ *Other:*	

(continued)

FIGURE **4.8** *Continued.*

○ If a laboratory experience is attached to the course, *go.* Take notes, ask questions, and be actively involved. Use the lab or field experience as a basis for understanding and remembering course concepts.

○ For laboratory work, record progress on experiments in real time so that you can review after class.

○ Preview the related lab assignment *before* the next class. This can help you better understand the lecture.

○ Add your own notes to PowerPoint and online lecture materials. Download and write on the hard copy during class.

○ Sit at the front of a classroom where you will encounter fewer distractions.

○ If your concentration fades during class, move your legs. Or, use your fingers to apply pressure to various stimulation points on your body—the back sides of your neck, top of your head, or area between your thumb and forefinger.

○ Add concrete and relevant explanations, examples, analogies, and case studies within your notes.

Tactile/Kinesthetic

○ After class, rewrite or retype your notes in order to simplify, reorganize, and summarize important ideas.

○ Move around when you review notes after class.

○ When reviewing notes after class, create a skit using terms, names, and other details that you need to know. Improvise by using zany associations within the skit, and act it out to reinforce remembering.

○ After class, summarize your notes by creating study cards with terms/concepts on the front and what they are associated with on the back.

○ As you review your notes, fill in concrete examples from the text or lab manual. Add practical applications, effects, or outcomes, as well as personal experiences related to the broader theories.

○ For answers to your questions, visit the instructor during office hours. For online course work, email your professor regularly.

○ *Other:*

Examples of students' Personal Action Statements.   FIGURE **4.9**

1. I will: reduce daydreaming during my history class.

2. My greatest hurdle to achieving this is: I get bored during class.

3. I will eliminate this hurdle by: (1) participating more during class—
   asking at least one question each class session; and (2) reviewing
   class material with my classmate Lisa each week.

4. My time frame for achieving this is: I will begin during tomorrow's class
   and evaluate when I meet with Lisa each week.

5. My reward for achieving this is: feeling like I'm not wasting my time
   during this class. Also, hopefully I'll be rewarded with a higher
   grade on my next quiz.

1. I will: highlight important ideas in my philosophy notes after each class.

2. My greatest hurdle to achieving this is: checking my email, Twitter,
   and Facebook.

3. I will eliminate this hurdle by: reviewing my notes for 15 to 20 minutes
   while I get a cup of coffee and THEN going online.

4. My time frame for achieving this is: to begin after my next philosophy
   class on Wednesday.

5. My reward for achieving this is: I'll see if this motivates me during
   the next week.

"I know reviewing class notes is important for learning. However, with a husband, a job, two aging parents, and household duties, I've always had problems finding the time. Lately I've done two things that have greatly helped: (1) Between classes, I review content by talking silently to myself, and (2) When I'm in the car, I review by listening to an audiotape of the lecture." —**KYLIE**

STUDENT VOICES

Your Personal Action Statement

1. I will: _____

   _____

   _____

2. My greatest hurdle to achieving this is: _____

   _____

   _____

3. I will eliminate this hurdle by: _____

   _____

   _____

4. My time frame for achieving this is: _____

   _____

   _____

5. My reward for achieving this is: _____

   _____

   _____

Conclusion

As your classes vary, so will your listening and note-taking techniques. New subjects and different instructors will spur you to alter how you best listen, take notes, and study for each course. As you assess and modify strategies, take into account this checklist of basic ingredients for successful and effective class listening and note taking:

Do...

- Go to all classes.
- Come rested and fed.
- Bring appropriate supplies: notebook paper, downloaded notes, and pens/pencils/highlighters or computer.
- Be familiar with the material to be covered in class.
- Sit in front, near the instructor and away from distractions.
- Listen actively; select ideas to write down on notepaper or type on your computer.

- If lecture notes are provided in advance, have them available during class to fill in information, add examples, and highlight important ideas.
- Create notes that are concise, clear, and accurate.
- Be alert; write/type, participate, and consciously *want* to pay attention.
- Adapt to your instructor's style and expectations.
- Review your notes *soon* after class while creating a study guide for yourself.

Don't...

- Write/type *every word* your instructor says or *only* words you see on the board.
- Copy classmates' notes or purchase ready-made notes in lieu of taking your own notes.
- Read online notes without *doing* something with them, i.e., picking out key points, highlighting and underlining ideas, adding examples, seeking clarification, and the like.
- Gripe about your instructor and complain about the class. Instead, put your energies toward positive outcomes by obtaining class information, completing assignments, and preparing for tests.

Comprehension Check

The notes in Figure 4.10 are from a class lecture about this chapter. Without looking back through the chapter, use these notes to create an after-class study guide that is complete and accurate. Use at least two of the strategies discussed in this chapter: Fill in incomplete information, add explanations and examples, highlight key words and phrases, summarize key points, and develop questions.

Reference

Pauk, W. (2001). *How to Study in College* (7th ed.). Boston: Houghton Mifflin.

FIGURE **4.10** *Comprehension check.*

	Date: _____
	CHAP. 4 ACTIVE LISTENING & NOTE TAKING
How alike?	Active listen'g is important because:
	Def. ⟶
How different?	
	Selective listen'g
	Def. ⟶
	Listening cues are important because:
Describe 2 types of listen'g cues.	
	Nonverbal cues are:
Give 3 examples of each.	
	Verbal cues are:

Summary:

Reading and Studying Text Material

FOCUS QUESTIONS

How can I better *understand* and *remember* what I read?

What are several recommended strategies before, during, and after reading?

Why is each strategy important?

CHAPTER TERMS

After reading this chapter, define (in your own words) and provide an example for each of the following terms:

- close-ended question words
- idea map
- open-ended question words
- previewing
- summary chart
- timeline
- visual study guide

Chapter 1	Chapter 2	Chapter 3	Chapter 4	Chapter 5	Chapter 6	Chapter 7	Chapter 8	Chapter 9
Academic Success	Managing Time	Being Productive	Active Listening	**Reading Textbooks**	Enhancing Memory	Test Preparation	Taking Tests	Continuing Success

Understanding and Remembering: Five Essential Ingredients

Can you identify with the following student?

Ted has to read Chapter 5 in his *Introduction to Psychology* textbook before tomorrow's class. He opens his text to the beginning of Chapter 5 and then heads to the end to count the pages. To his dismay, the chapter is 30 pages long! He gets out his blue highlighter pen and highlights sentences and paragraphs that, as his eyes move across the page, he thinks are important. He reaches the end of the chapter about an hour later. "Whew, I'm done with that assignment," Ted thinks as he contentedly closes his textbook, expecting to reopen it three weeks from now when he will reread all the blue sections of the pages in preparation for the midterm exam.

However, if someone were to ask Ted to summarize what he just read about in Chapter 5, he would not be able to do it. In fact, the next day in the psychology lecture, Ted was not at all familiar with the terms and ideas that the professor was talking about, even though this material was covered in Chapter 5 of the text. In reality, all Ted accomplished the night before was to create 30 blue pages! He had no understanding, let alone recall, of the important ideas presented in the text chapter.

Ted's method for reading the text material is all too universal. Many students feel a sense of accomplishment with getting the task done—that is, going through the pages—without obtaining a true understanding of what they are reading. If you fall into that category, strategies for reading and studying do exist that can increase both your understanding *and* recall of important information. These strategies are suitable and adaptable for traditional textbooks, novels, and articles as well as electronic books and Web-based reading assignments.

Critical Thinking Task

pause... *and reflect*

Describe yourself as a reader—that is, characterize your usual approach to a reading assignment. Consider these points:

YOUR READING BEHAVIORS: WHAT YOU DO WHEN YOU HAVE AN ASSIGNMENT

- Do you tend to read the assignment immediately or to procrastinate?
- Do you prepare or organize yourself *before* reading? For instance, do you skim through the assignment or look at the end-of-chapter questions or numbers of pages?

- As you read, what do you do? Do you read the whole assignment in one sitting, or do you take frequent breaks? Do you write on hard-copy text or add notes to an electronic text? Do you highlight, take separate notes, or answer study guide questions?
- Are you able to concentrate when reading? How do you keep your mind focused?
- *Afterward*, do you review what you read? If so, how? Do you reread the entire assignment? Do you quiz yourself?

YOUR ATTITUDE TOWARD READING ASSIGNMENTS

- Are you generally motivated to begin the assignment?
- Do you persist, even if you think the content is boring or difficult to understand?
- Do you often avoid reading? Do you dislike reading? Why?

YOUR PREFERENCES WHEN READING

- When reading, do you prefer complete silence, or do you prefer music or background noise?
- How long can you read and still maintain your focus: 10 minutes, half an hour, or how long? How about breaks? Do you need to move around frequently when reading? Do you tend to move your mouth or hear yourself read?
- When reading, do you concentrate best at a particular location and time of day?
- Do you prefer to read and study from a traditional hard-copy book or electronic version? Why?

ONLINE COURSE WORK

Many texts are available in both hard-copy and online versions. When given a choice between the two, consider the factors in Figure 5.1.

You likely will discover that the reading demands for your college courses will be unlike what you have previously encountered. Instructors will expect you to read larger amounts and differing types of materials independently. You will be required to combine reading with class notes, understand complex ideas in print, and analyze multiple sources for discussion and writings. This type of reading, termed *study reading*, demands a high level of comprehension. To be effective, the process you employ for study reading should result in understanding

| FIGURE **5.1** | *Hard copy versus electronic copy.* |

	HARD COPY	**ELECTRONIC COPY**
Advantages	• Use own handwriting and colorful highlighting to help you comprehend content. • Easier to move back and forth among pages and illustrations. • No interruptions from online distractions, including embedded hyperlinks. • More likely to achieve deeper level understanding of content when reading hard copy as opposed to online text. • Campus bookstores or other vendors buy back certain textbooks, though for varying prices.	• Very portable. • Less expensive than hard copy. • Often you can choose whether to buy or to rent for a set amount of time. • Easy to store and access for future use. • Most e-book readers let you download annotations, notes, and portions of the text to form a self-study guide. • Features and add-ons make e-text more adaptable, such as changing and enlarging fonts, text-to-speech, and translations into other languages. • Environmentally friendly.
Disadvantages	• More expensive. • Used copies are less expensive, but might be wrong edition, not have packaged supplements, or be filled with distracting markings from the previous owner. • Heavier to carry. • Takes up storage space.	• Not always available. • More difficult to preview the reading material and get an overview of content. • More difficult to flip among pages and create colorful highlighting and annotations—all of which help understanding and recall of text material. • Built-in distractions of embedded hyperlinks, videos, and Web sites. • More difficult to achieve deeper level of understanding when reading online text.

and then recall of important information. The following five steps will guide you toward maximum effectiveness and efficiency in understanding and remembering what you read. Apply these steps when reading hard-copy books and articles, as well as online materials.

1. Preview what's ahead.
2. Break up your reading.
3. Check your understanding.
4. Create study guides.
5. Review periodically.

Preview What's Ahead

Previewing will assist you with learning new, and often complex, information contained in reading assignments. Previewing means getting a quick picture of the whole before proceeding with the detailed parts of a chapter or article. The more familiar you are with any subject or idea, the more likely you will understand it. Familiarize yourself with both the topic and layout of the assignment. The previewing step is a way to build a strong, familiar framework for understanding and remembering new material. In addition, the few minutes you spend previewing can greatly improve your concentration while reading.

GET AN OVERVIEW OF THE BOOK

What parts of a textbook can you glance at to become familiar with the content? The table of contents is important because it presents the overall organization of the book. Also, skim through the preface, introduction, copyright, index, appendixes, and answer keys. You need only do this step once: before you begin reading the first chapter assignment. This quick initial step will provide you with a general idea of the overall layout of the text, the organization of content, the author's viewpoint, and any text-related aids to assist you when reading.

try it out!

Preview a textbook that you are using this term. After previewing, you should be able to answer these questions:

- What are the key components of the text?
- What is the general organization of content?
- How difficult does the text seem to be?
- What related guides, CDs, or Web sites are available?

GET AN OVERVIEW OF THE CHAPTER OR ARTICLE

You want to gain some familiarity with a chapter or article you are about to read. *Previewing* means flipping through pages and glancing at the characteristics of the chapter, including headings, subheadings, introductions, summaries, questions, length, vocabulary/terminology, graphics, spacing, and overall layout. Once you are acquainted with the topics, organization, and difficulty level of the chapter/article, you are prepared to read for both understanding and recall.

try *it out!*

To understand the benefits of previewing, open your text to a new chapter. Allow yourself *one minute* to flip through (or scroll down, if using a computer) the pages and note characteristics of the chapter, such as the headings, subheadings, questions, summary, and so on. At the end of a minute, close the text and recite to yourself what you just found out about the chapter. Nothing is too insignificant to note.

You likely will recall information about the chapter's topics and content as well as details about the format, such as the length, graphics, and difficulty level. Most students are surprised about how much information can be gleaned from a chapter in a minute; this information will provide you with a familiar context from which to begin your reading of the assignment.

IDENTIFY YOUR PURPOSE

Why are you reading this chapter? What are you going to do with the information? Your purpose for reading helps you identify how much and what type of information you need to know. If your purpose is to use the information for class discussion, you only need to read to understand the main concepts in the chapter. If your purpose is to do well on the upcoming 100-point test, you will need to read for main ideas as well as for lots of supporting ideas and details. A 10-point quiz on the chapter content means you will need to read primarily for main ideas. Be clear about what types of questions you will be asked and how much detail you are expected to know. Thus, for peak reading efficiency, be clear as to *why* you are reading and *how much* information you need to know.

Break Up Your Reading

For maximum effectiveness, read one section of a chapter or article at a time. Reading a section at a time makes sense because the author has already divided the material into paragraphs around a common topic; therefore, you should take advantage of these divisions. After reading the section, stop and ask yourself, "What are the key ideas?" If you honestly cannot identify the important ideas, go back and reread the section.

Sometimes reading an entire section at once is too much. If the material is difficult and complicated, you might need to read one paragraph at a time to understand the subject matter fully. Or, if the section is quite long, you may need to divide it up and read several paragraphs before stopping and checking for comprehension. However, do *not* break up your reading into chunks that are too small. Stopping too frequently will make reading tedious and time consuming, and it can chop up ideas to the point that the material doesn't flow and doesn't make sense to you.

ONLINE COURSE WORK

Hyperlinks within text are among the many distractions associated with online reading. When you click on the many links, you break up your reading to the point that your concentration and comprehension falter. Keep in mind that each time you open a link, you are pulling your attention and your thoughts *away from* the main text. Therefore, the rule of thumb is to open hyperlinks *after* you have read one or more sections of a chapter or article.

Check Your Understanding

Reading is a thought process that involves figuring out what is important, what you need to know, and how you will use the information. Asking questions enhances this thought process by focusing your attention on key ideas and the connections among these ideas. Your questions will stimulate thought and help you to create meaning from text. After reading a section, stop and check your understanding by answering questions about the main topic of the passage:

Critical
thinking
task

- What are distinguishing characteristics of this topic?
- What are key terms associated with this topic?
- What are significant changes that developed as a result of this topic?
- What are the connections between this and another topic?
- Who are the key individuals associated with this topic?
- What conclusions can I draw about this topic?
- What's important for me to know about this topic?
- How will I use information about this topic for this course?
- What confuses me about this topic?

Reading to discover the answers to these and similar questions focuses your attention, promotes thinking, and ultimately helps you develop meaning out of the written text. To maximize your comprehension of the passage, answer the questions in your own words.

Create Study Guides

ombining reading with studying is an effective and efficient technique. Unlike Ted, described at the beginning of this chapter, do not separate the two. As you check your understanding of the passage, write, type, or highlight points to remember.

- Answer questions.
- Paraphrase key ideas.
- Add details and explanations.
- Provide concrete examples and meaningful situations.

By writing, typing, or highlighting important points, you will be (1) immediately reinforcing the information, and (2) developing a study guide for later review.

You have choices as to the type of study guide you can create. Your decision depends on your purpose for reading, your background and familiarity with the subject, the difficulty level of the text, and what you need to know for the upcoming quiz, exam, or discussion. The purpose of a study guide is to help you select, organize, understand, and remember key information for your course.

An effective study guide presents information in an organized, concise manner and helps you learn and recall text information. The intent of a study guide is to maximize both the effectiveness and the efficiency by which you study for your courses. Types of study guides that are useful for college students are described on the following pages.

QUESTION-AND-ANSWER STUDY GUIDE

Three words that are key to increasing your reading comprehension and concentration are *what*, *why*, and *how*. These are termed **open-ended question words** because they generate answers that are broader and more conceptual than do the other three question words: *who*, *when*, and *where*. The answers to what, why, and how tend to be *main ideas*. The answers to who, when, and where, in contrast, tend to be *specific facts*, which is the reason they are termed **close-ended question words.**

For the question-and-answer study guide, you develop questions to guide your reading; that is, you read to discover the answers to questions. If the chapter or article that you are reading contains headings, use the headings as a basis for creating questions. Otherwise, create your own questions. To focus on main ideas and concepts, use what, why, and how questions. If you need to know details for tests, add who, when, and where questions. After reading a section, think about—and write or type—the answer to each question. Write your question and accompanying answer in the text, on a separate sheet of paper, or on index cards, or type them on the computer for later self-testing.

Figure 5.2 provides an example of study guide questions created from chapter headings. By creating questions and then answering the questions, you will be actively identifying important ideas within a section and thus becoming a more focused reader. In addition, you will have developed a question-and-answer study guide for later review.

Example of study guide questions.   FIGURE 5.2

1. heading: <u>The Steps of the Scientific Method</u>

   question: What are the steps of the scientific method?

2. heading: <u>Forming a Hypothesis</u>

   question: How should I form a hypothesis?

3. heading: <u>The Importance of Observation</u>

   question: Why is observation an important part of the scientific method?

4. heading: <u>The Baroque Era of Music</u>

   questions: What are the major characteristics of baroque music?

   Who were the major composers during the era?

   When did the baroque period begin and end?

"I used to just jump in and read. Now, I begin by reading the introduction and conclusion; this gives me a general idea of what I will be reading. Also, I change headings into questions and try to answer those questions to see how much I comprehend. These are the best habits that I've gotten into." —SHI-ANN

"When I have a chapter to read, the first thing I do is turn all headings and subheadings into questions. I also look for italicized and boldfaced words and turn them into questions. I then skim through the section, looking for the answer. This greatly cuts down on both the time it takes me to read and unnecessary note taking." —DENNIS

STUDENT VOICES

HIGHLIGHTING-PLUS-MARKING STUDY GUIDE

The advantage of highlighting and underlining is that you can emphasize important ideas in the text without rewriting the ideas on a separate sheet of paper. Consider these factors when highlighting.

1. **Read first and then highlight.** If you highlight *as* you read, it is difficult to distinguish important from unimportant ideas. Also, because ideas are often repeated within a section, you tend to overhighlight if you don't read the material first. In addition, highlighting while you read can disrupt concentration. Instead, read the section first, and then use highlighting as a means to check your understanding of key ideas.

2. **Highlight as little as possible to get the idea across.** Most students err on the side of overhighlighting—that is, they think nearly everything is important. This defeats the purpose of a study guide; if you emphasize too much, you end up rereading most of the chapter or article. Instead, focus on key words or phrases that get the idea across. Avoid highlighting whole sentences or, worse yet, whole paragraphs. If everything in a paragraph is noteworthy, use markings to emphasize *what* and *why* the information is important.

The advantage of adding markings on a page is that you are not limited to just the words used in the text. Markings help make important ideas clearer and more distinct. Such markings include:

- *Summarizing* a passage with a short phrase [e.g., "visual learn'g preferences"].
- Indicating the *organization* of material [e.g., (1) (2) (3)].
- Using *symbols* to *emphasize* ideas [e.g., +, >, →, *].
- Indicating *why ideas are important to know* [e.g., "How am I a visual learner?"].

Markings combined with highlighting or underlining create an effective study guide because you are *interacting* with the text material, making ideas as explicit as possible. Figure 5.3 provides an example of a highlighting-plus-marking study guide.

ONLINE COURSE WORK

You can create a highlighting-plus-marking study guide with digital text. Tablet personal computers come with a growing number of tools and applications that allow you to write on the screen, create notes and flash cards, and the like. Also, e-book readers have functions that allow you to highlight, bookmark, and add notes. Afterward you can download your annotations and clipped sections of the text to form a self-study guide. *Caution:* Do not select the automatic highlighting option on your e-book reader—instead, *you* choose which ideas to highlight.

Example of highlighting plus marking.   FIGURE **5.3**

---

visual learn'g preferences

Bio. Prof.
Dr. Ada Worth is a visual learner and, therefore, relies on visual strategies and
　　　　　　　3 ex. of tchng. strategies
materials when teaching her biology classes. For lectures, she writes most of the
　　　　　(1)　　　　　　　　　　　　　　(2)
ideas on the board and often uses the overhead projector. Also, she gives students
　　(3)　　　　　　　3 ex. of student expectations
handouts illustrating material covered in each class. Furthermore, she wants
　　　　　　　　　(1)
students to use the mapping format of note taking to summarize articles discussed
　　　　　　　　　　　　　　　　　(2)
in class. Finally, she expects students to keep their lab areas free of clutter and to
　　　(3)
write neat, clear notes in their lab manuals.

* How am I a visual lrner??

OUTLINING STUDY GUIDE

You likely are familiar with the standard format for outlining a passage: organizing notes by writing main ideas to the left with supporting ideas underneath, indenting to the right as ideas become less general and more detailed. Outlining is most effective if you paraphrase ideas presented in the text—that is, if you write or type key points in *your own words*, adding explanations or examples. In Figure 5.4, note the use of action words to begin the phrases in the outline.

STUDY CARDS

Study cards are especially effective when you need to know terms and definitions, including examples and applications of the terms. The front of an index card showcases a name, term, concept, or main idea. Putting the term or idea in a question format helps you focus on what you need to know. For instance, if you are reading about the scientific method, on the front of your study card write, "What are steps of the scientific method?" On the back, write the

FIGURE 5.4   *Example of outlining.*

Dr. Ada Worth is a visual learner and, therefore, relies on visual strategies and materials when teaching her biology classes. For lectures, she writes most of the ideas on the board and often uses the overhead projector. Also, she gives students handouts illustrating material covered in each class. She wants students to use the mapping format of note taking to summarize articles discussed in class. Finally, she expects students to keep their lab areas free of clutter and to write neat, clear notes in their lab manuals.

I. Dr. Worth ———→ visual lrnr./instructor
   A. Lecture techniques
      1. Writes on board
      2. Uses overhead projector
   B. Provides handouts
   C. Uses mapping
   D. Lab expectations
      1. Neat environment
      2. Neat student notes

definition, explanation, example, or other appropriate details. Be concise and use your own words.

An advantage of study cards is that you must be *selective* when reading a text because you are separating text information into individual parts for the front and back of the cards. Study cards can help you pinpoint main ideas and related details in the text. In addition, study cards are excellent tools for quizzing yourself orally and teaching others. Create study cards if you want *repetitive* reinforcement of text information.

However, a disadvantage of study cards is the tendency for students to memorize, as opposed to learn, the information. Study cards generally are not effective for in-depth analysis and synthesis of text material. Figure 5.5 shows two examples of study cards.

Examples of study cards.   FIGURE 5.5

FRONTS

What are <u>sedimentary</u> rocks?

Why important?

What are <u>metamorphic</u> rocks?

Why important?

BACKS

— Made of particles;
   fragments cemented together.

— Gives clues to ancient
   environment & climates.

— Any igneous or sed. rock that is
   burned; changes form.

— Gives clues about plate
   tectonics.

VISUAL STUDY GUIDES: MAPS, CHARTS, AND TIMELINES

Most people learn and recall best when they can visualize information. Idea maps, summary charts, and timelines are all visual summaries of ideas in print. A **visual study guide** involves *active reading* of text material to

1. Identify key ideas—both major and minor—in the text passage.
2. Identify relationships among these ideas.
3. Create an organized, concise summary.

   Reading to fill in a map, chart, or timeline can be an efficient method of reading a text. First, identify the overall relationships among ideas in the passage and create a frame for your chart or map. By first recognizing the categories

"I *never* marked books—it was not allowed. Even today, if I make a stray mark or accidentally bend a page, I am appalled at my own carelessness! I recently realized that my attitude needs to change if I am to survive as a college student; I am learning to value books in a different way. Lately, I've been underlining important ideas, and so far the book hasn't self-destructed!" —NICOLE

"In the past, textbook reading seemed a waste of time. I would think, 'Why read the textbook when the professor gives us notes?' However, it was impossible for me to excel this way, so I started reading and highlighting. At first I was highlighting *everything* in the chapter. I was reading chapters two or three times because I thought everything was important, which is why I got bored when reading. Since then, I have highlighted *words*, not entire sentences. This has helped me to slow down and understand more precisely what I am reading. Also, I discovered that marking in the margins makes the important points stand out so that they catch my eye." —GAVIN

"Often, the class material and book material are parallel. Thus I read the chapter *before* class so that I can more easily keep up with the instructor's lecture. I bring my book notes to class and mark in the margins what the instructor goes over so I know what to study for a test. I always mark examples used in class; examples make great memory joggers in the middle of a 'blank out' during a test. In addition, if I have a question in class, I see if I can answer it myself by first referring to my book notes." —KATE

"I've grown accustomed to buying digital versions of my books, especially those needed for my major courses. They are less costly and easy to access. I especially like the highlighting function; I click on a link to create a summary of my highlighting." —MEGHAL

or types of information you need to know, you will be eliminating unneeded information when reading the text. Then read to complete the study guide. This technique of reading to fill in a chart, map, or timeline can speed up your reading and thus is an efficient reading strategy.

Furthermore, visual guides are excellent tools to use for review before exams. To create a visual study guide, you will be organizing, categorizing, and simplifying text information, all of which result in *knowing* the material. The concise visual image provides a perfect format for speedy overviews before a test. A number of computer programs are available that enable you to create a variety of visual study guides.

Models of visual study guides include the following:

- **Idea maps** (Figure 5.6) are especially appropriate for showing the connections among main ideas and subordinate supporting ideas.
- **Summary charts** (Figure 5.7) present an effective framework for summarizing and categorizing key features, including definitions, characteristics, accompanying examples, and relationships.
- **Timelines** (Figure 5.8) are suitable for material organized in chronological order, such as a progression of events or steps in a process.

Four examples of idea maps.   FIGURE **5.6**

I. The **topic** (*1960s Protest Movements*) is divided into *three* **main ideas,** each of which has offshoots—**supporting ideas** with **details.** Note the parallel placement of the supporting ideas with similar themes: 1) which phase of the movement, and 2) people.

(continued)

FIGURE **5.6**   *Continued.*

II. The **topic** (*"STUDY CARDS for reading"*) is divided into two distinct **categories** (*"ADVANTAGES"* & *"DISADVANTAGES"*):

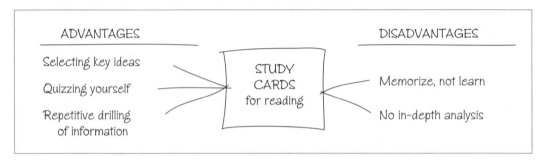

III. This idea map presents the two parts ("active" vs. "inactive") related to the topic ("quiet breathing"):

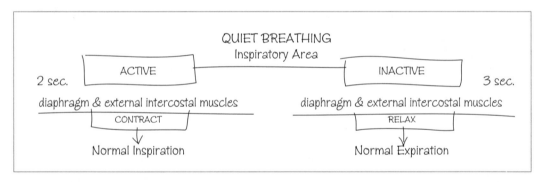

IV. This idea map illustrates a **cause-and-effect** relationship among ideas. The topic is "THE INDUSTRIAL REVOLUTION":

Two examples of summary charts.   FIGURE **5.7**

PSYCHOLOGICAL DISORDERS

TYPES	DEFINITION	EXAMPLES	FEELINGS
Anxiety	Characterized by distressing, persistent anxiety	1) Panic attacks—last several minutes; intense dread 2) Phobias—fears	Chest pain, choking, smothering sensation, rapid heartbeat
Somatoform	Symptoms take solo form w/ no physical cause	1) Conversion disorder—anxiety is converted into physical symptoms 2) Hypochondria—interrupts normal sensations	Dizziness, vomiting, blurred vision
Dissociative	Conscious awareness becomes separated from memories	1) Amnesia—failure to recall events 2) Fugue—fleeing one's home & identity for days/months	Facing trauma, forgot what was intolerable, painful, the way they should act or feel
Mood	Emotional extremes	1) Major depression—prolonged depression 2) Bipolar disorder—alternates between depression and mania	Lack of energy, not able to eat/sleep normally, better off dead; much pressure

(continued)

FIGURE **5.7** *Continued.*

Cause-and-Effect Chart for Civil Rights Movement

CAUSE	EFFECT
Southern closed society	– Blacks excluded from politics – Whites controlled economy – Segregation is the norm
13th Amendment	– Ends slavery
14th Amendment	– Nobody can be processed without due process
15th Amendment	– Black men allowed to vote
Jim Crow laws	– Revokes blacks of all their rights
Plessy v. Ferguson 1896	– Establishes doctrine "separate but equal"
Black soldiers returning from WWII	– Demanded jobs (learned skills during war) and desegregation
Brown v. Board of Education (1954)	– Most important civil rights case – Ruled unanimously that "separate but equal" is not equal
Southern manifesto	– 100 congressmen oppose desegregation – Say it violates the Constitution and the 14th Amendment
Montgomery bus boycott	– Strong black community – MLK Jr. put into national role – Combination of legal strategies and nonviolent direct action – Protest begins the movement – SCLC is formed

[Created by Melissa Swope]

Two examples of timelines.   FIGURE 5.8

Feminist Movement

Time Period: Goals, Accomplishments, & Characteristics:

| 1st Wave | 1848–1950's |

1. 1848: Start of Women's suffrage movement. Delegates to Women's Rights Convention, Seneca Falls, NY, adopted Declaration of Sentiments. 1st public demand for women's independ. Supporters insulted, assaulted, &/or ignored by pop. press & leaders.
2. 1900: Suffragists publicly marched protesting for right to vote.
3. 1920: Women received right to vote.
4. Break from women's traditional roles of dependency & submission.

| 2nd Wave | 1960s–1980s |

1. Women's continuing social, legal, & financial independence & self-direction.
2. Enlightenment of options in & out of home.
3. "Equal Pay for Equal Work."
4. Opening doors in nontraditional workplaces.
5. Reproductive choices & freedoms.
6. Primarily involved white middle-class women.

| 3rd Wave | 1990s–21st Century |

1. Breaking the so-called glass ceiling to top positions within workplaces.
2. Addressing race & class inequalities.
3. Overcoming domestic violence & rape.
4. Rights of homosexuals & transgendered people.
5. Broadening scope of feminism.
6. Focus feminism on daily practicality, as opposed to theory & intellectuality.

(continued)

FIGURE **5.8**   *Continued.*

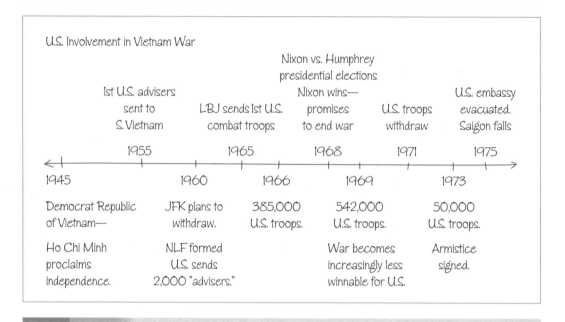

U.S. Involvement in Vietnam War

	Nixon vs. Humphrey presidential elections		
1st U.S. advisers sent to S. Vietnam	LBJ sends 1st U.S. combat troops	Nixon wins— promises to end war	U.S. troops withdraw	U.S. embassy evacuated. Saigon falls

1955   1965   1968   1971   1975
←|————|————|————|————|————|————|————|————→
1945   1960   1966   1969   1973

Democrat Republic of Vietnam—

Ho Chi Minh proclaims independence.

JFK plans to withdraw.

NLF formed U.S. sends 2,000 "advisers."

385,000 U.S. troops.

542,000 U.S. troops.

War becomes increasingly less winnable for U.S.

50,000 U.S. troops.

Armistice signed.

Review Periodically

At least once a week, look over your study guide. This regular review keeps the many and varied pieces of information rooted in your memory. Here are some approaches for weekly review.

ADD OR COMBINE LECTURE MATERIAL

Are there parts of the text that help clarify complex ideas from the lecture or vice versa? Can you identify overlapping text and lecture information, information that likely will be on a future exam? Can you see how parts of the text and lecture relate to one another and combine to form an image of the whole?

TALK ALOUD

As you review, say the information aloud, either to yourself or to another person. Use as many of your senses as possible to learn and remember the new information—*see* the information in your study guide, *say* the information aloud, and *hear* yourself, thus reinforcing the subject matter. If possible, teach someone else as you review; find a friend, classmate, or family member who will listen and ask questions as you explain the information. If you are able to clearly *teach* it to another person, you likely *know* it.

ANTICIPATE TEST QUESTIONS

Predict and write down questions you expect to appear on the upcoming quiz or exam. This tactic will help you be selective with quantities of information. Also, you will be thinking of the information in terms of immediate use—that is, knowing it for the test.

Here are the steps for reading an assignment effectively and efficiently:

1. Preview to obtain a general idea of what's ahead.
2. Read a section.

3. Check your comprehension.
      If "YES"   If "NO"
4. Create your study guide.
5. Review periodically to help you remember.

try it out!

Critical Thinking Task

Using your current course assignments, create and use the various types of study guides. After using each study guide, **Assess Your Success** by writing its advantages and disadvantages on Figure 5.9. Use the following four questions to guide you as you judge the value and drawbacks of each type of study guide:

1. Does this study guide assist me to *understand* the content as I read?
2. Does this study guide help keep my attention *focused* on what I am reading?
3. Does this study guide assist me to *remember* important information?
4. Is this study guide a worthwhile tool for *review* before a test?

FIGURE **5.9**   *Assessing study guides.*

STUDY GUIDE	ADVANTAGES	DISADVANTAGES
Question and Answer		
Highlighting plus Marking		
Outlining		
Study Cards		
Idea Map		
Summary Chart		
Timeline		

try it out!

Critical Thinking Task

Learning Modalities, Strategies, and Reading/Studying

1. In Figure 5.10, Reading and Studying Strategies are categorized as predominantly involving visual, auditory, or tactile/kinesthetic modalities. Place checks in the circles next to those strategies that you *do use regularly*.
2. Choose a strategy that you do *not* use consistently but that would likely help you with an upcoming reading assignment.
3. Write a Personal Action Statement for that strategy.
4. After completing the strategy, refer back to your Personal Action Statement and **Assess Your Success:**

   • Did you accomplish what you set out to do? Explain.
   • Describe how you were able to overcome any obstacles.
   • Think about your experience and how successful you were with understanding and remembering what you read. What additional behaviors or different techniques can you implement to make your system of reading and study effective and efficient for *you*? Incorporate these new strategies in a Personal Action Statement for your next reading assignment.

Reading and studying strategies and learning modalities. FIGURE 5.10

READING AND STUDYING STRATEGIES   LEARNING MODALITIES

○ To help your comprehension, get an overview *before* reading. Look at the introduction, headings, and summary.

○ When reading, *focus on main ideas first* (look at the first and last sentences; read the summary) to understand the big picture. Then, go back and read more carefully for details.

○ When reading, focus on seeing relationships or organization of ideas. Use symbols such as arrows and marginal notations that show the relationships of ideas within a passage.

○ For longer passages, break up your reading by using highlighters and colored pens for visual emphasis. Use color-coded tabs to separate topics and chapters.

Visual

○ Create visual study guides: Organize text information by creating an *idea map* relating main ideas with details. Or develop a *chart* that illustrates key names/terms and accompanying characteristics or details. Or develop a *timeline* of key events.

○ Color-code your highlighting according to type of content. For example, use green for important terms, pink for important people, blue if the information was reviewed in class, and yellow for general knowledge. This can be especially useful for social science textbooks.

○ For terms, make colorful study cards with the term on the front and a brief explanation on the back.

○ *Other:*

○ Especially for complex and important information, heighten your comprehension by talking aloud as you read so that you hear yourself.

○ Class lectures and discussion are often your strength, so use class information as a basis for understanding the text. Review lecture notes before reading. Keep notes handy as you read, thinking about how class information fits into text readings.

○ Use audiotapes, following along as you read. Or create a tape of yourself reading out loud.

Auditory

○ Participate in group study and review sessions to *discuss* text information. Compare and contrast your study guides with others'.

○ Teach others; this will reinforce what you *know* about subjects.

○ Use supplemental materials on companion Web sites, videos, or CDs that provide auditory reinforcement.

○ *Other:*

(continued)

FIGURE **5.10**   *Continued.*

READING AND STUDYING STRATEGIES	LEARNING MODALITIES

○ If you procrastinate with reading, join a collaborative study group. If you know others are depending on you, you will be less likely to put off reading an assignment.

○ *If you prefer variety and action, speed up your reading:* **(1)** focus on the first and last sentences of paragraphs; **(2)** use chapter headings as guides to identify main ideas; **(3)** create a study guide by turning headings into questions, then read to answer the questions.

○ Pace around the room as you read, or act out what you are reading.

○ A hard copy textbook (as opposed to e-text) allows you to more readily flip among pages and add notations.

Tactile/Kinesthetic

○ Move your fingers across the page as you read.

○ Make associations between new information and real-life experiences—as you read, jot down the associations. Use lab and field work as a means to strengthen your understanding of written material.

○ Read for short chunks of time, taking regular breaks where you move about.

○ Use supplemental materials on companion Web sites or CDs that provide animated three-dimensional experiments and demonstrations.

○ *Other:*

Conclusion

BEFORE YOU READ

- **Know why you are reading the material.** What are you going to do with the information? Are you taking a short quiz, a longer exam, or an essay test, or is this information for class discussion? Tailor your reading to fit the purpose of each assignment.
- **Get an overview of the chapter or article.**
  - Skim over headings, italicized and boldfaced print, the introduction, the summary, and the questions at the end.
  - Note the order and difficulty level of material.
  - Anticipate how long you will need to read for an understanding of the information.

DURING YOUR READING

- **Break up your reading and check for comprehension.** Reading section-by-section helps keep your concentration high and your mind focused.
- **Think about what is important to know.** If you read to discover ideas, you will increase your understanding of the material.
- **Create a study guide.** This should reflect what you need to know for the upcoming exam or discussion.

"Surveying helps me see what the author is trying to teach. I make my own questions and try to answer them; this helps keep me interested in the reading. Reciting my answers helps me know if I really understand what I am reading. Constant review has saved me from forgetting (which I'm a real expert at doing)." —PATRICE

STUDENT VOICES

AFTER YOU READ

- **Review your study guides weekly.**
  - Review the text with the lecture.
  - Talk aloud.
  - Anticipate test questions.

See Figure 5.11 for a summary of study guides.

Comprehension Check

eturn to the focus questions on page 75. Jot down an answer for each question as if you were creating a question-and-answer study guide or answer the questions as an outlining study guide.

For each chapter term make a study card; write the term on the front and your definition and example on the back. Or, complete a three-column summary chart with these three headings: Term, Definition, and Example.

FIGURE **5.11**   *Summary of study guides.*

Description	Advantages	Disadvantages
QUESTIONS AND ANSWERS		
Develop questions from headings/subheadings; Then *read to discover the answers.*	• Predicting questions will increase your reading comprehension. • *What, why, how* questions direct your attention to *key ideas,* thus increasing concentration while reading. • You tend to read faster; this is beneficial for a *large amount* of reading.	• By reading *just* to answer a question, you could be missing other key ideas. • Not effective when careful, detailed reading is necessary.
HIGHLIGHTING *PLUS* MARKING		
After reading a section, *highlight words* or *phrases* representing key ideas. *Add markings* to summarize, organize, and/or emphasize important information.	• Beneficial if you need to know *much text information,* that is, main ideas *plus* details. • An effective and convenient method of *emphasizing ideas* right on the page.	• Effectiveness is greatly reduced if you highlight *too much* or *too little* or if you don't add markings. • Can consume more time than other types of study guides.
OUTLINING		
Write key points in your own words; indent for progressive details. Add explanations or examples.	• Effective if you prefer to *rewrite information* for maximum recall. • Worthwhile if you prefer to learn material in a *linear format.*	• By just rewriting boldfaced headings and subheadings, you will create an easy, but *ineffective,* study guide.
STUDY CARDS		
On front, write question, term, concept, or main idea. *On back,* write definition, explanation, example, or supporting details.	• Especially effective for recall of *terms and definitions.* • Separates information into individual parts. • An easy format for oral quizzes.	• Tendency to *memorize* as opposed to *learning* new info. • Difficult to show effectively how ideas are related or organized.
VISUAL GUIDES—*Maps, Charts, Timelines*		
A concise summary that indicates how ideas are organized or related. A variety of formats: chart, idea map, or timeline.	• Forms a *visual* picture of written material, which increases recall. • An *efficient* way to read: when you "fill in" the frame of the chart or map you created, you eliminate unneeded information.	• Can be difficult or confusing, especially if you are unused to identifying relationships among ideas. • Limits the amount of detail that can be included.

Your Personal Action Statement

Identify a reading assignment: _____

1. I will: _____

    _____

    _____

2. My greatest hurdle to achieving this is: _____

    _____

    _____

3. I will eliminate this hurdle by: _____

    _____

    _____

4. My time plan for achieving this is: _____

    _____

    _____

5. My reward for achieving this is: _____

    _____

    _____

Reference

Carr, N. (2010). *The Shallows: What the Internet Is Doing to Our Brains.*
New York: W. W. Norton & Company, Inc.

Enhancing Your Learning and Memory

FOCUS QUESTIONS

Seven essential ingredients are presented in this chapter. Prioritize them from the most important for you to work on to the least important.

How are sleep, time management, and memory connected?

Describe a situation in which you used your senses to enhance your memory.

CHAPTER TERMS

After reading this chapter, define (in your own words) and provide an example for each of the following terms:

- association
- collaborative learning
- mnemonic device
- visualization

Chapter 1	Chapter 2	Chapter 3	Chapter 4	Chapter 5	Chapter 6	Chapter 7	Chapter 8	Chapter 9
Academic Success	Managing Time	Being Productive	Active Listening	Reading Textbooks	**Enhancing Memory**	Test Preparation	Taking Tests	Continuing Success

Learning and Memory: Seven Essential Ingredients

Regrettably, a magical formula to boost one's learning and memory does not exist. It is the commonsense study habits and strategies, implemented consistently, that strengthen understanding and recall. Many of these strategies were described in Chapters 2 through 5. This chapter highlights seven fundamental ingredients to increase learning and improve memory:

1. Get enough sleep.
2. Study in small, regular blocks of time.
3. Review soon after receiving new information.
4. Organize and categorize information.
5. Study with others.
6. Use your senses.
7. Associate ideas.

Get Enough Sleep

Regular, adequate nighttime sleep is a critical element of learning. For college students, insufficient sleep is a major reason for poor recall. Research studies confirm the far-reaching and damaging effect that lack of sleep has on learning, performance, and memory. By maintaining seven to nine hours of uninterrupted sleep nightly, you will greatly enhance your thinking ability and capacity to recall information.

In addition, daytime naps of 20 to 60 minutes can improve your overall sense of well-being, as well as your academic performance. Research studies using magnetic resonance imaging (MRI) scans of the brain demonstrate how midday naps can improve brain functioning and revive mental alertness, as illustrated by Eve's experience (see nearby "Student Voices").

STUDENT VOICES

"Three or four days a week, I take what I refer to as a *power nap*. A power nap is lying down and sleeping for an hour in the afternoon. If I sleep more than one hour, I wake up feeling tired, not refreshed. Since I work until 2 a.m. some mornings and never get the same amount of sleep every night, these power naps are important to me." —EVE

The bottom line is that a well-rested student understands and remembers more and therefore performs better than the sleep-deprived student.

Study in Small, Regular Blocks of Time

Your memory will be clearer at the beginning and at the end of any task or situation; it is the middle section that often becomes muddled and less clear. For instance, you likely remember the beginning stage of high school when you were a new freshman going into an unfamiliar building, meeting new teachers, having new challenges, and so forth. In addition, the last part of your high school experiences—your senior year—likely provides memorable impressions in your mind. The middle years tend to be less distinct and more tangled.

Also consider the amount of time for study sessions. Most people lose their mental energy and concentration after 30 to 60 minutes; thus, plan accordingly. You can increase your mental acuity by simply dividing one long study session into shorter sessions of no more than an hour. Take a short break between sessions by switching activities. This change of activities provides your brain with time to rest, to reflect, and to process the information that, in turn, strengthens your recollection. (*Note*: This strategy also applies when scheduling classes: You likely will learn and remember more in three one-hour class sessions per week as opposed to one three-hour class session.)

Therefore, a method of increasing your memory is to study information in small blocks of time with a short break between sessions. The blocks of study time that you set aside for an assignment depend on certain factors:

- **Subject Matter.** Most students are able to concentrate for longer periods of time when working with material they find interesting or relevant.
- **Difficulty Level.** Most students are able to concentrate for longer periods of time when the information is not so difficult as to cause frustration nor so easy as to cause boredom.
- **Time of Day.** Students stay focused longer when they are feeling fresh and alert.

Plan ahead and consider the factors just listed when scheduling blocks of time for study and review.

Review Soon After Receiving New Information

Repetition embeds information in the mind and therefore is key to learning and recall. Begin reviewing *soon* after your initial exposure to the information so you don't have to relearn the subject matter.

"I found out that most people retain only about 20% of what they sup-posedly learned during the day. Therefore, rereading my class notes at night has been a good idea; it works as reinforcement. I also review my textbook material more frequently. This has made test preparation go a lot easier and quicker for me. Plus, there are fewer things on the test that do not look familiar." —BEN

Organize and Categorize Information

Critical Thinking Task

The more you can establish relationships among ideas, the more you tend to remember the ideas. Linking or grouping information will enhance your understanding and recall of the subject matter. For example, a student studying for an upcoming quiz in a biology class created the summary chart in Figure 6.1. Note the three distinct categories and four parallel phases under each category. This student created an organized framework by which to remember key information.

FIGURE **6.1** *Example of organizing and categorizing.*

MITOSIS	MEIOSIS I	MEIOSIS II
Prophase:	Prophase I:	Prophase II:
Metaphase:	Metaphase I:	Metaphase II:
Anaphase:	Anaphase I:	Anaphase II:
Telophase:	Telophase I:	Telophase II:

Study with Others

Collaborative learning is when two or more students pool their efforts and resources to work together on an academic task. In collaborative learning settings students help each other understand course content by asking and answering questions, explaining concepts, solving problems, providing examples, and offering mutual support. Learning collaboratively can greatly strengthen your understanding and remembering of content, particularly content that is intellectually challenging and complex. You might have access to collaborative study groups on your campus; many institutions offer structured study/review groups for students enrolled in courses with traditionally difficult content. Trained peer leaders guide small groups of students on how to learn new and difficult course content. Common names for these course-based groups are Supplemental Instruction, Peer-Led Team Learning, Peer-Assisted Learning, Structured Learning Assistance, and the like. Also, many college tutorial programs are set up so that students, with the guidance of trained tutors, work collectively on learning course content. If ready-made collaborative learning groups are available, do go; participating regularly throughout the semester can greatly improve your learning, memory, and grade for the course.

If collaborative groups are not available for a course, create your own study group. Here are steps that will help you lay the groundwork for an effective study group.

1. Select suitable classmates. The ideal size of a study group is two to five people; all should be responsible, be task-oriented, and have the common goal of achieving a relatively high grade in the targeted course.

2. Choose a suitable location where you can talk without interruption, spread out materials, and, if possible, have a board to write on. Consider study rooms in a library, an empty classroom or lounge, or a room in someone's apartment or home.

3. At the start agree on expectations and practices for the group. Members should:

   - Commit to an active role *preparing for* the study session by completing assigned problems, reading the chapters, reviewing class notes, and the like.

   - Commit to an active role *during* the study session by asking questions, clarifying content, solving problems, practicing test questions, teaching the material to each other, and creating study guides. (You don't want one or two members carrying the weight for others.)

   - Pay attention when others are talking (turn off mobile devices).

   - Strive for an atmosphere of easy give-and-take among people. A positive, supportive atmosphere will increase the motivation and productivity of members.

   - Keep breaks short. Be mindful of when you get ·off track and then quickly rebound toward work.

By incorporating these practices from the start, you are more likely to have an efficient and successful study group.

ONLINE COURSE WORK

For online courses, seek collaborative learning opportunities within online discussion groups and chat rooms. Decide on a common day and a time slot, usually 30–60 minutes. As with a face-to-face study group, agree on expectations and practices (it is more difficult to monitor participation within online groups). During the allotted time, members should be prepared to ask and answer questions and share practice problems and sample test questions.

Use Your Senses

Review information regularly, using as many of your senses and modalities as possible. The more hands-on multisensory activities you employ, the more likely you are to retain the information.

STUDENT VOICES

"If I write something out on paper, I am more likely to remember it. For reading assignments, I write down important ideas in my notebook next to class notes referring to the same topic. If needed, I will draw pictures or diagrams from the book into my notes. By combining a text chapter with class notes, I am able to see the whole picture at once. I am enjoying the feeling of really *knowing* the material." —**NIKITA**

"When a professor puts a lot of information and complicated problems on the board, I use my cell phone to take a picture at the end of the class. Then I can check the photo against my notes and fill in the areas that I've missed." —**RAVI**

- **Seeing.** Create visual pictures, and illustrate and color-code ideas. **Visualization,** forming a mental picture, is a vital component of memory. By visualizing information, you will be implanting images in your mind and thus retaining more. For instance, for a geoscience course, a student created an organized framework with several visual emphases; she added gradients and differences in lettering as well as a column to sketch each type of stress/fault (see Figure 6.2).

Example of visualization.   FIGURE 6.2

Type of STRESS	What It Does	Type of FAULT	Example	SKETCH
EXTENSIONAL	Stretches and tries to pull the rock layers apart	NORMAL	Death Valley	
COMPRESSIONAL	Smashes and tries to push the rock layers together	REVERSE/THRUST	Grand Tetons	
SHEAR	Tears and tries to slide rocks past one another	STRIKE SLIP	San Andreas	

[Created by Heather Kline]

- **Saying.** Talk to yourself. Teach others. Join a study group to orally review and discuss the subject matter.
- **Hearing.** Recite aloud to hear the information. Again, studying with others will provide opportunities to listen to people talking about the subject matter.
- **Touching.** Use your sense of touch to emphasize shapes, textures, and contours of materials. For example, for a geology course, try feeling different types of rocks or tracing the outlines of geological formations.
- **Doing.** Write down information, act out scenarios, play a game, or simply move about while reciting information. For example, students in a study group for a general psychology course played charades when trying to remember psychological disorders. They acted out the various types of disorders while others guessed the name of the disorder and corresponding treatment. Reviewing information using a similar action game can make a profound and lasting impact on your memory.

pause.... *and reflect*

The first six ingredients for enhancing memory—(1) get adequate sleep; (2) study in small, regular blocks of time; (3) review soon after receiving new information; (4) organize and categorize; (5) study with others; and (6) use your senses—were presented in previous chapters.

1. Refer to Chapter 2, "Managing Your Time," and reconsider the elements of sleep and regular blocks of study time.
    *   To improve your memory skills, where should you make changes?
    *   Should you increase sleep by going to bed earlier, inserting power naps, or other alterations in your schedule?

2. Refer to Chapter 4, "Active Listening and Note Taking," and reevaluate your habits.
    *   Should you add review time soon after certain classes to improve your learning?
    *   What do you do with your lecture notes to enhance your understanding and, ultimately, recall of important information?
    *   Do you need to create more or different study guides for lecture notes to improve your memory of key information?

3. Refer to the "Visual Study Guides: Maps, Charts, and Timelines" section of Chapter 5, "Reading and Studying Text Material" (p. 87). Development of a visual study guide involves identifying and organizing key ideas within a visual format; thus maps, summary charts, and timelines often enhance retention.
    *   How often do you create and use visual study guides when reading?
    *   How about when preparing for an exam? Have you developed a study guide that summarizes course material in a concise visual format?
    *   Describe a map, chart, or timeline that was effective in improving your recall in a particular subject.

4. Have you participated in collaborative learning situations? Which of your courses have small-group study/review sessions or tutoring sessions? If you have participated, how helpful have the sessions been? If you have not participated, why not? Have you been involved in other study groups, either face-to-face or online? How helpful have they been?

Associate Ideas

Association means relating or linking new information to that with which you already know. By connecting *new* ideas with familiar ideas already rooted in your mind, you can form memorable images to boost immediate recall. Be inventive and unique when linking ideas together; silly, exaggerated, or bizarre associations will produce lasting remembrances.

Association is often employed for short-term recall of facts and details that you tend to forget because the information is complex, unfamiliar, meaningless, or without context. For example, a student in a chemistry course created the following association to help her remember the details of the structure of the atom:

> "Visualize an **atom** as an *apartment building*: an atom has many different **shells** and an apartment building has many different *floors*. Each shell has **subshells**, and each floor holds *apartments* of differing sizes. The apartments are collections of *rooms*, and the **subshells** are collections of orbitals."

> —Carly M. Solazzo

ritical
hinking
ask

pause... *and reflect*

Mnemonic devices are another type of memory tool best used for short-term recall of details. An effective mnemonic device is simple to devise and easy to remember. The disadvantages of mnemonic devices include the following:

1. You are *remembering*, not *learning*, information.
2. They can be cumbersome to create and easily confused when you most want to remember details accurately and clearly, that is, when taking the test!

EXAMPLES OF MNEMONIC DEVICES

1. Creating a catchy rhyme, jingle, or song:
   - Remembering specific biology researchers and types of cells each studied: "People go slipping and **Schliden** on **Plant** cells and **Schwann** (swan) for **Animal** cells."
   - Remembering number of days for each month: "Thirty days has September, April, June, and November; all the rest have 31, except February, which has 28."

2. Using the first letters of words to develop a word or phrase:
   - A campus building: *Hadley Union Building* = "HUB"
   - Piaget's Stages of Cognitive Development:

     Sheila (Sensorimotor)

     and

     Peter (Preoperational)

     Counted (Concrete operational)

     Frogs (Formal operational)

When have you used mnemonic devices to remember details? Describe several situations to share with classmates.

try *it out!*

Learning Modalities, Strategies, and Learning/Memory

To strengthen your learning and memory employ multiple strategies and modalities.

1. In Figure 6.3, Learning and Memory Strategies are categorized as predominantly involving visual, auditory, or tactile/kinesthetic modalities. Place checks in the circles next to those strategies that you *do use regularly*.
2. Next, identify a strategy that you do *not* use consistently but which would likely help improve your learning and memory in your course work.
3. Write a Personal Action Statement showing how you will apply the strategy in a course this week.

Critical Thinking Task

4. After completing the strategy, refer back to your Personal Action Statement and **Assess Your Success:**

   - Did you accomplish what you set out to do? Explain.
   - Describe how you were able to overcome any obstacles.
   - Think about your experience and how successful you were with understanding and remembering. What additional behaviors or different techniques can you implement?

Learning and memory strategies and modalities.

FIGURE 6.3

LEARNING AND MEMORY STRATEGIES	LEARNING MODALITIES
○ Visualize information in your mind. Strengthen your recall by imagining that you see the information.	
○ Make color-coded study cards, especially for terms. Use symbols and illustrations to help you visualize the information.	
○ Use sticky notes as visual reminders. Place the notes in accessible locations, such as on your computer, bathroom mirror, refrigerator, or front door.	**Visual**
○ To remember steps for a problem or process, such as with math and science course work, develop a flowchart or diagram that separates each step.	
○ Create mnemonic devices by using the first letters of words to develop a new word or phrase that you can visualize.	
○ *Other:*	
○ Recite aloud while reviewing.	
○ Talk and interact with others to improve memory.	
○ Create a catchy rhyme, jingle, or song as a memory technique.	
○ To remember steps for a problem or process, such as with math and science course work, talk out loud as you move through each step.	**Auditory**
○ To strengthen recall, imagine hearing the information.	
○ *Other:*	
○ To strengthen memory, use all of your senses: sight, touch, taste, smell, and hearing.	
○ Move about and read aloud while reviewing.	
○ Whenever possible create three-dimensional models of information.	
○ Act out roles, play charades, and develop games. Create a skit using terms, names, and other details that you need to remember. Improvise by using zany associations within the skit and act it out to reinforce remembering.	**Tactile/Kinesthetic**
○ To remember steps for a problem or process, such as with math and science course work, use index cards for each step. Arrange the cards in the correct order.	
○ To strengthen recall of abstract concepts, imagine related lab experiments, computer programs, field trips, photographs, and the like.	
○ *Other:*	

Your Personal Action Statement

1. I will: _____

   _____

2. My greatest hurdle to achieving this is: _____

   _____

3. I will eliminate this hurdle by: _____

   _____

4. My time plan for achieving this is: _____

   _____

5. My reward for achieving this is: _____

   _____

Conclusion

The grid in Figure 6.4 lists the memory techniques presented in this chapter. As part of the end-of-chapter comprehension check, summarize the techniques by completing the chart: Add a description of the strategy, an example of how you've used it, and comments regarding its effectiveness. Add other strategies at the bottom.

Comprehension Check

1. Employ the technique of visualization by creating an illustration that answers the following question: "How are sleep, time management, learning, and memory connected?"
2. Describe a situation in which you used your senses to enhance your memory.

Summary grid.   FIGURE 6.4

MEMORY STRATEGY	DESCRIPTION	EXAMPLE	COMMENTS
Adequate sleep			
Small blocks of time			
Review soon after			
Organize/ categorize			
Study with others			
Use your senses			
Association			
Mnemonic devices			
Other			

C H A P T E R   7

Preparing for Tests

FOCUS QUESTIONS

How are test-taking anxiety, test preparation, and test-taking performance related?

Compare and contrast preparation for objective tests versus essay tests.

CHAPTER TERMS

After reading this chapter, define (in your own words) and provide an example for each of the following terms:

- cumulative final exam
- deep muscle relaxation
- desensitization
- mental imagery
- mental trigger
- performance anxiety
- test anxiety

Chapter 1	Chapter 2	Chapter 3	Chapter 4	Chapter 5	Chapter 6	Chapter 7	Chapter 8	Chapter 9
Academic Success	Managing Time	Being Productive	Active Listening	Reading Textbooks	Enhancing Memory	**Test Preparation**	Taking Tests	Continuing Success

Success with Tests: Be Prepared

KEEP UP WITH ACADEMIC WORK

Test preparation starts from the first day of the semester. For both face-to-face and online courses maintaining regular study *throughout each week* is a crucial element of test preparation. The more complex the information, the more time you will need to process and understand course content adequately for an exam. If you have followed strategies suggested in previous chapters, you likely are ready to study (as opposed to cram) for the upcoming exam:

- Have you attended all classes and taken appropriate notes?
- Have you sought information about class sessions or assignments that you missed or were unsure about?
- Have you reviewed your notes soon after each class—clarifying, organizing, emphasizing, and summarizing key ideas?
- Have you kept pace with reading assignments, creating some type of study guide that represents important ideas?
- Have you reviewed weekly, with a classmate, tutor, or study group, in an online discussion, or by yourself?

If you answered yes to all or most of these questions, you have been integrating study with day-to-day academic demands and thus are well prepared for the next step: *reviewing* and *consolidating* subject matter before the exam.

DEVELOP TEST REVIEW GUIDES

Plan for added study time each day during the week before a major test. During this added time, select, combine, and organize key information from class notes and readings and create concise review guides. Look for the major topics, often repeated in both readings and class notes; then dissect these major topics into related subtopics. Think about how the topics are connected. For example,

- Topic A is *part of* topic B.
- Topic A is *the opposite of* topic B.
- Topic A *results in* topic B.
- Topic B is *an example of* topic A.
- Topic B *describes* topic A.
- Topic B is *a function of* topic A.

Study cards to review for psychology test.   FIGURE **7.1**

OBSERVATION	Study behavior in natural setting. Adv: normal setting Disadv: no cause/effect
CASE STUDIES	Info. gathered about specific individuals. Adv: detailed Disadv: a lot of time

Because test items often reflect these topics and connections, make sure they are part of your study guide, as illustrated here and on the following pages.

Study cards (Figure 7.1) are useful when you expect to have many terms or concepts on an upcoming test. On an index card, write the term or concept on the front and a summary, definition, explanation, or other associated ideas on the back. Study cards are effective for test review because they are handy and flexible; use them to review while waiting in line, between classes or appointments, in a bus or car, and so on.

Maps and charts (Figure 7.2) are effective tools for test review because they help you select, organize, and categorize important ideas and details in a visual format—key strategies for enhancing your recall of information.

REHEARSE FOR THE EXAM

Practice test questions. Prepare for an upcoming exam by answering questions similar to the types of questions that you expect to be on the test. By completing practice questions, you are reviewing the subject matter while familiarizing yourself

FIGURE **7.2** *Review chart for history test.*

"VIETNAM: Progression of Events"

Vietnam Events	WHAT is it?/WHY important?	WHO?	WHEN?
Domino Theory (escalation)	Like row of dominoes—if one country falls, so will the rest.	Eisenhower	1954
Dien Bien Phu (escalation)	French troops parachute into a fort; terrible loss; only 200 of 1,400 escape.	French	1954
"Flexible Response" (escalation)	2,000 "advisors" going to Vietnam to research what is going on.	JFK	1960
Gulf of Tonkin (escalation)	Advises the president to take "all necessary measures."	LBJ	Aug. 1964
Tet Offensive (escalation)	Widens the scope of the war.		1968
"Peace with Honor" (withdrawal)	Nixon's election slogan—take U.S. troops out of Vietnam w/ honor.	Nixon	Nov. 1968
My Lai Massacre (withdrawal)	Public outrage w/ revelations that U.S. soldiers massacre 500 noncombative civilians.	U.S. soldiers; Charlie Team; William Calley	March 1968 breaks in Dec.
The Pentagon Papers (withdrawal)	Reveals everything about the war.	Daniel Ellsberg	June 1971

[Contributed by Melissa Swope]

with the format of the test (i.e., essay, multiple choice, true/false, matching, identification, and/or sentence completion questions). Use the end-of-chapter or separate study guide questions, or create your own practice questions. If you participate in a study group, ask each person to make up practice questions to share with the others.

Teach others. An additional type of rehearsal is to run through the material by teaching the information to another person. When you are able to explain information clearly to others, you likely know it. Convince a roommate, family

ONLINE COURSE WORK

Reproduce the online testing format as much as possible:

- Rehearse reading and analyzing test questions on a computer screen. Some courses and textbook packets have accompanying online practice tests. If not, develop your own test; place questions on your computer to simulate the type of test you will be taking for the course.
- If you will be taking tests in a computer lab, practice in that lab or a similar lab so that you become comfortable with the test-taking environment.
- For timed tests, practice with time constraints to build your speed and confidence for the real exam.
- If on the real test you won't be able to go backward/forward or skip items, practice taking tests with these same restrictions.

"I am an English major; thus keeping up with the reading is of utmost importance. Most importantly, I try to attend all of my classes because a large part of the test questions seem to come straight from class sessions. The week before the test, I usually have the bulk of all material read, which leaves the last several days for review, reinforcement, and mini-quizzes. Lately, I have been feeling more confident about my learning, and my test scores reflect this." —KESHIA

STUDENT VOICES

member, or friend to be the designated student, or teach the material to yourself. In the role of teacher you will be training yourself to know the information thoroughly. At the very least, saying the information out loud will help reinforce what you do and do not know.

Finally, **cumulative final exams** cover content that has been covered throughout the semester (as opposed to an exam covering content for a shorter span of time). Because of the quantity of material to study, preparing for a cumulative final exam can be especially challenging. Here are several additional strategies to help you prepare for a cumulative final exam:

- Study previous quizzes and tests. This will help you review both content covered and types of questions on tests for this course. Also, sometimes instructors repeat specific—or similar—test questions on the final exam.

"First, I allow myself four to five days to study for a test. Second, I anticipate what questions may be on a test, and finally I find a family member to 'teach' the subject matter to. By using these three strategies I have already increased my grades in two classes." —SAM

- The majority of questions on cumulative exams tend to cover content from the latter portion of the semester—that is, content that you have not yet been tested on. Therefore, prepare accordingly; make sure to allot plenty of study time for the most recent course material.
- Do attend review sessions, especially those led by the instructor. Or, see the instructor during office hours. Come prepared; ask for clarification about confusing content, suggestions for how to study for this exam, and sample test items.

try it out!

1. Identify a *subject* in which you will be having a major exam in the near future.
2. In *preparation* for the exam, answer the following questions:
   - When is the exam?
   - What topics and material are to be covered in the exam?
   - What types of questions will be on the exam?
   - Have you been keeping up with course work for this subject? If not, where have you been falling behind and what do you still need to do?
3. Continue preparing for the exam by creating a *test review guide*, either study cards or a map or chart.
4. Next, develop a *practice exam*, using questions similar to the type you expect to be on the real exam.
5. Continue *rehearsing* for the exam by teaching key concepts to another person.

6. After you have taken the exam, **Assess Your Success** with the methods of preparation you used for this test.
   - Which preparation strategies did you find to be especially effective and why?
   - Which strategies were *not* effective for you? Why?
   - How will you approach preparation for the next exam in this subject?

Reduce Test Anxiety

DO YOU HAVE TEST ANXIETY?

Preparation is a key factor in reducing extreme worry and anxiousness associated with taking a test. However, at times, even the best prepared student gets trapped in a cycle of excessive anxiety. **Test anxiety,** a type of **performance anxiety,** is based on the apprehensive thoughts and emotional feelings associated with how well you will do on an exam.

Consider this example: Two people look outside and see bright sunlight. One person thinks, "Great weather! I can't wait to go swimming today!" He feels lively and full of energy. Another person sees the same bright sunlight but thinks, "Darn it—I have to water the grass and flowers again today." He feels lethargic and moves slowly. These two people have completely different thoughts—and subsequent physical feelings—about the same situation.

Similarly, people have differences in thoughts and physical reactions in regard to test taking. One student might think of an exam as a personal challenge, whereas another thinks of the same exam as a personal threat. It is the latter student who worries, often excessively, about the test and, as a consequence, often exhibits physical symptoms of anxiety.

your THOUGHTS [worry]

↓ lead to ↓

your PHYSICAL REACTION [anxiety]

Test-taking anxiety is a condition that interferes with positive test results. How anxious are you when taking a test? Would you have performed better if you weren't so uneasy and fearful? This next "Try It Out!" will provide an estimate of your level of test anxiety.

try it out!

Test Anxiety Assessment

Complete by checking *Yes*, *Sometimes*, or *No* for each of the twelve statements:

WHEN PREPARING FOR OR TAKING A TEST:	YES	SOMETIMES	NO
1. I think about whether I'm going to pass or fail.	✓	○	○
2. I keep wishing the exam were over.	✓	○	○
3. I worry that I am not doing well.	✓	○	○
4. I can't stop thinking about how nervous I feel.	○	○	✓
5. My stomach gets upset.	○	○	✓
6. My heart beats very fast.	○	○	✓
7. I often freeze up, and my mind goes blank.	○	✓	○
8. I feel hot and sweaty.	○	○	✓
9. I feel very tense.	○	○	✓
10. I forget information that I really know.	○	✓	○
11. I often get panicky.	○	✓	○
12. I tend to breathe faster.	○	○	✓

SCORING – Total your points using the following key:

Each *Yes* = 2 points
Each *Sometimes* = 1 point
Each *No* = 0 points
Your total points = ___9___

(You'll have a total score between 0 and 24.)

The higher your total score on the Test Anxiety Assessment, the more anxious you are when taking a test. If your score is between 10 and 24, you'll likely benefit from working on strategies to reduce the worry and anxiety associated with test taking.

Note that items 1 through 4 on the questionnaire refer to those thoughts that impact negatively on your test-taking performance. Worry over your test results, whether you are going to pass the course, whether you will make it through college, or even your family members' reactions can interfere with test performance. Excessive worry can lead to a physical reaction toward test taking, including sweaty palms, rapid breathing, dizziness, and so on. Assessment items 5 through 12 refer to this physical response. Thus apprehension plus a physiological response results in full-blown test anxiety.

Keep in mind that not all worry and anxiety is bad. In fact, *some* anxiousness can be good in that it keeps your adrenaline flowing and, as a result, gives you that edge to perform better. However, you do not want your anxiety to be excessive to the point where it interferes with your performance. If you think that you could have done better on a test if you weren't so anxious, you need to tackle ways to reduce this anxiety.

Critical Thinking Task

pause... *and reflect*

Refer back to your total score on the Test Anxiety Assessment.

- If your total score is less than 10: Reflect about why your anxiety is low. Consider how you approach a test—that is, how you *think* about exams and what you *do* that keeps anxiety at a minimum. Why don't you worry excessively?
- If your total score is 10 or above: Think about those *situations* that trigger worry and anxiety for you. Here are some circumstances that might set off anxiousness:

  - The word *test* on the syllabus or board.
  - The night before the exam.
  - The morning of the exam.
  - Walking into the classroom or computer lab to take the exam.
  - Other students discussing the exam.
  - The instructor distributing the exam.
  - A test item that you're not sure how to answer.
  - Waiting to get the results.

Come up with at least three or four scenarios that apply to you. Beside each scenario, write the *exact thoughts* that run through your mind when you are in that situation. For example, for the situation "A test item that you're not sure how to answer," you might have these thoughts: "Oh no, I'm going to fail!" or "I should know this answer," or "This is terrible!"

CHANGE HOW YOU THINK ABOUT THE TEST

One way to diminish feelings of test anxiety is to change your thoughts about tests.

Focus on the *present*, not the past or the future. Test-anxious students tend to focus their thoughts on what occurred previously ("I did poorly on the last quiz") or what they predict to occur ("I'm going to fail this test"). Bear in mind that your past performance does *not* foretell your present performance. Likewise, you cannot predict accurately what the outcome of a test will be. Therefore, keep your thoughts focused on the here and now—that is, your present place in time. Be alert to the thoughts that run through your head; if you begin to think about past or future events, *stop* and redirect your thoughts to what you are doing or can do *now*. Deter yourself from thinking about an imaginary future and, instead, think about the realistic present moment in time. For example,

"I did poorly on the last chemistry quiz and am going to fail this upcoming quiz."

↓ changes to ↓

"I am doing practice problems in anticipation of the next chemistry quiz."

Put the test in perspective. Test-anxious students tend to overinflate the importance of any single test. In the realm of worldly events, any one exam is not *that* important! Keep a realistic, less extreme perspective about quizzes and tests. Students sometimes are helped by playing out, in their minds, a frightening chain of events linked to test performance. This tactic produces scenarios that often are exaggerated and ridiculous. As an example, the following is the chain of thoughts for one anxious student:

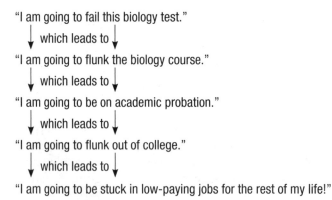

"I am going to fail this biology test."

↓ which leads to ↓

"I am going to flunk the biology course."

↓ which leads to ↓

"I am going to be on academic probation."

↓ which leads to ↓

"I am going to flunk out of college."

↓ which leads to ↓

"I am going to be stuck in low-paying jobs for the rest of my life!"

Ideally this student realizes that it is neither logical nor realistic to think that failing a biology test will result in a lifetime of low-paying jobs. Being aware of unreasonable thinking patterns can help you maintain a more balanced view of a test.

Recognize your choices. "I *have to* do well" or "I *must* get an A" are common thoughts of students fretting over a test. These thoughts imply that the student has no other options *but* to perform well—or even perfectly! Practice eliminating the phrases "have to," "required to," "should," and "must" from your thoughts. Instead, replace them with phrases that suggest you have options, such as "I *prefer to* do well" or "I'd *rather* improve my score on the next exam." Mindfully choose words that evoke personal choices and the leeway and sense of freedom that come with these choices.

Be positive. Be alert to your negative, and even apathetic, thoughts. Instead, focus on positive, encouraging aspects of yourself and your actions. Choose words that reflect optimism and personal affirmation. Also, seek encouragement from family and friends. As a result, you will feel more upbeat and confident about taking tests. For example,

"I'm so angry at myself for getting a C on this quiz!"

↓ is replaced with ↓

"It's *okay* that I received a C; I'll probably *improve* on the next quiz."

"I don't care what I do on this test!"

↓ is replaced with ↓

"I will try to earn a *reasonable* grade on this test."

critical thinking task

pause... *and reflect*

Do you see yourself reflected in any of these thought patterns? Refer back to page 125, where you identified specific thoughts associated with testing situations. Using the previous suggestions for changing how you think about a test, create *new* statements to reflect a change in your own thought pattern.

CHANGE HOW YOU REACT PHYSICALLY TO A TEST

Because test-anxious students view the exam as threatening, their bodies react as in any other intimidating or frightening situation: Breathing becomes more shallow and rapid, the heart beats faster, muscles tense, adrenaline flows throughout the body, skin becomes sweaty, and digestion slows down. This physical reaction is appropriate when a situation is actually threatening, such as spotting an animal running in front of your car when you are driving. In that situation it *is* appropriate that your body becomes tense as you focus only on not hitting the animal. However, these same intense physical symptoms work *against* you when taking a test; tense muscles, rapid breathing, upset stomach, and so forth can cause you to lose your concentration and mental acuity. Instead of focusing on the content of the exam, you become focused on your extreme and even frightening physical reactions. However, by using two simple techniques—**mental imagery** and **deep muscle relaxation**—you can greatly alter your physical response to a test.

Mental imagery. Your mind plays a powerful role in determining your physical response to an event. A calm, peaceful image in your mind can result in a tranquil, stress-free physical response. Think of an event in your own past that evokes a feeling of personal contentment, joy, or satisfaction. Use all of your senses to reconstruct a realistic version of this event. Imagine yourself in that situation: What are you specifically doing? What sounds do you hear? What are you saying? Can you smell or taste anything? What are you feeling? Because this situation activates a feeling of calm and contentment within you, it is called your **mental trigger.** Use this mental trigger often. Become accustomed to generating this mental image to prompt a response of easy relaxation.

Deep breathing and muscle relaxation. You likely tense your muscles when a stressful, threatening situation arises. This tense, rigid bodily response can rapidly lead to feelings of panic, which result in poor test performance. With directed practice, you can train yourself how to replace the tense response with a calming response.

"Since I'm usually well prepared for exams, you'd think that I'd be more relaxed come exam time. I just can't seem to walk into a room, knowing I'm going to take a test, and be calm. Deep breathing does help—some. I take a couple of breaths before I walk into the test room (at least I know I'm still breathing, right?). I think I'm hopeless, so the thing I do is talk to myself, which I've become a pro at. I just try to put each test into perspective. I point out that I am prepared, I've studied, and that one test won't blow my grade. This helps to bring me from 'high-strung' to just plain 'nervous,' but this isn't all bad. I think it's the perfectionist's advantage, being able to handle a nervous, pressure situation." —RACHEL

One type of deep muscle relaxation exercise begins with monitoring your breathing so you are mindful of slow, full, even breaths that originate deep in your abdomen (as opposed to shallow breaths originating in your upper chest). Do this exercise when you have a chunk of time by yourself, in a darkened, quiet room, with your eyes closed. Next, focus on relaxing your muscles from the top of your head down through the trunk of your body, to your limbs, to your fingers and toes. Concentrate on one group of muscles at a time, letting these muscles become loose and relaxed. Picture your muscles becoming heavy, like a wet mop. By loosening your muscles, you will be calming your body. With practice over time, you will be able to create this feeling of deep relaxation easily and quickly and, as a result, free your mind to concentrate on tasks such as preparing for or taking an exam.

DESENSITIZE YOURSELF

Desensitization refers to a gradual, yet steady exposure to the anxiety-producing event. Desensitization begins by breaking down the event—in this case, test taking—into small and specific anxiety-producing situations. You place the situations in order: from *least* to *most* anxiety producing. Starting with the situation creating the least anxiety, you combine mental imagery (imagining yourself in the particular situation) with deep muscle relaxation techniques. Monitor your physical responses while you practice mentally being in the specific situation. Build toward real exposure of the test-taking situation; continue to monitor both your mental and physical reactions.

As an example, one student identified the following scenarios as producing varying levels of personal anxiety:

> "I have some anxiousness when I hear the instructor announce the date of the test. I then worry every time I see the word *test* in my planner. My anxiety really increases a few days before the test when I begin to study more. I have trouble sleeping the night before a major test. The peak of my anxiety is when I enter the classroom the day of the test!"

This student's anxiety builds for each succeeding scenario. For desensitization, the student begins with the *least anxiety-producing scenario:* "the instructor announces the date of the test." While in a state of deep muscle relaxation, the student creates a mental image of being in a specific classroom and hearing the instructor announce a test date. The student rehearses thought patterns that counter anxiety, such as "I'll prepare for this test the best that I can." The student repeats this image and related thoughts until he notices that his response is continually calm. At this point, he continues with desensitization by imagining the *next higher scenario:* "seeing the word *test* in my planner." He continues until his calm, relaxed responses readily translate to real-life test scenarios.

"Taking a test used to be one of my worst nightmares; I had almost every symptom of test anxiety. I used to get so mad for allowing myself to get so upset. I created so much pressure for myself, including whether I would pass or fail, how low my GPA was, that the instructor hated me, how dumb I felt, I should have studied more, etc.—all of which affected the way I took a test. I was so relieved to find ways to overcome the fear of a test.

The first improvement I made was to complete my studying on a daily basis, instead of cramming during an all-night study binge. By covering the material regularly, I don't feel the need to cram, and my anxiety has greatly diminished. I begin preparing for a test by reviewing my notes several days in advance. Now, when reviewing I am able to recall important ideas readily, which makes studying less of a problem. If I do begin to feel tense, I relax myself by taking deep breaths. This permits me to feel more comfortable with taking a test." —SHANA

Critical Thinking Task

pause... *and reflect*

1. Refer to Figure 7.3. In the left-hand column, place a check mark in the circle beside each of the listed situations that result in some level of worry or anxiety for you.
2. Order the circles with check marks, from least anxiety producing (write a 1 on the line next to that circle) to most anxiety producing.
3. To the right of each item with a check mark, write at least one way you can reduce anxiety by changing your thoughts, your actions, and/or your preparation techniques.

Reducing test anxiety.

FIGURE 7.3

Causes of Test Worry and Anxiety	Ways to Reduce or Eliminate
○ _____ The first test of the semester.	
○ _____ The test counts toward a big chunk of the final grade.	
○ _____ The test covers lots of material.	
○ _____ I don't fully understand the material.	
○ _____ I don't feel prepared for the test.	
○ _____ I don't feel competent with the type of questions.	
○ _____ I allowed too little time for studying for the test.	
○ _____ I am taking more than one test during the day.	
○ _____ I've previously performed poorly in the course.	
○ _____ I'm afraid that I'm going to forget key information.	
○ _____ I feel pressure to get a good grade in the course.	
○ _____ I'm thinking about my family's or instructor's expectations.	
○ _____ I'm concerned about my overall GPA.	
○ _____ I'm afraid of failing.	
○ _____ I'm concerned about my future job prospects.	
○ _____ Any other?	

try *it out!*

Practice reducing anxiety you might have about an upcoming quiz or test.

1. Use *mental imagery*. In your mind, identify and recreate a scene that triggers a sense of calmness.
2. Combine your mental image with *deep muscle relaxation*. Practice breathing and relaxing all of your muscles systematically. Do this exercise at least twice a day for 15- to 30-minute sessions when you are able to turn off lights, be comfortable, and not be disturbed by others.
3. Practice *desensitization*. Begin with the least anxiety-producing situation that you previously identified.

Critical Thinking Task

4. **Assess Your Success** by answering the following questions:
   • How have you progressed with the process just described? Explain your progress with each step.
   • After completing a test or quiz, have you noticed a reduction in your worry and anxiety? Describe the test-taking situation and your reaction.
   • What will you continue to do to decrease your anxiety?

try *it out!*

Learning Modalities, Strategies, and Test Preparation

The following steps will help you choose strategies to best prepare for an exam:

1. In Figure 7.4, Test Preparation Strategies are categorized as predominantly involving visual, auditory, or tactile/kinesthetic modalities. Place checks in the circles next to those strategies that you *do use regularly*.
2. Next, identify a strategy that you do *not* use consistently but which would likely help you prepare for your next quiz or test.
3. Write a Personal Action Statement for that strategy.

Critical Thinking Task

4. After taking the test **Assess Your Success:**
   • Did you follow through and reward yourself accordingly? Explain.
   • Did the hurdle materialize and did you manage it effectively? Explain.
   • What other changes do you want to make before your next quiz or exam?

Test preparation strategies and learning modalities.   FIGURE **7.4**

TEST PREPARATION STRATEGIES	LEARNING MODALITIES
○ Develop a visual plan indicating times, places, and materials needed for studying. ○ So that you are better able to form a mental picture of information, choose a study location away from others and free of distractions. ○ Develop test review guides that organize and categorize information, such as an idea map, timeline, chart, or graph. ○ If the exam consists of essay questions, use models of sample answers for practice. ○ Create visual cues for information that you anticipate needing to know for an exam. ○ To remember steps for a problem or process, develop a flowchart or diagram that separates each step. ○ *Other:*	**Visual**
○ Create a catchy rhyme, jingle, or song as a memory technique. ○ Attend review sessions or peer tutoring. Ask questions and participate in discussion. ○ *Teach others* the material; this will reinforce what you know. Or, debate others as a method of reviewing information. ○ To remember steps for a problem or process, talk out loud through each step. ○ To help remember details, use the first letters of words to develop a word or phrase and say it repeatedly out loud to yourself. ○ *Other:*	**Auditory**
○ Develop a written plan with times, places, and methods for studying. ○ Use a study location with adequate space to spread out. ○ Pace and move about while studying. Have a worry stone or stress ball in your hand. ○ Practice using your fingers to apply pressure to various relaxation points on your body—the area between your eyebrows, behind your earlobes, and tops of your wrists. ○ Schedule extra practice and study time in a laboratory setting. Seek out case studies, computer programs, lab experiments, and/or photographs as a means to understand complex terms and abstract concepts.	**Tactile/Kinesthetic**

(continued)

FIGURE **7.4** *Continued.*

- Use role-playing as a means to review for exams. Present the information to a classmate or family member. Create a "game show" that reviews information.
- Create three-dimensional models as a means of review.
- Use blackboards or whiteboards to develop practice test items, make graphic representations of information, or play a game on the board with classmates.
- Replicate the testing situation and *practice*. For online tests, use a computer, go to a lab, and time yourself.
- *Other:*

Your Personal Action Statement

Identify an upcoming test: _____

1. I will: _____

   _____

   _____

2. My greatest hurdle to achieving this is: _____

   _____

   _____

3. I will eliminate this hurdle by: _____

   _____

   _____

4. My time frame for achieving this is: _____

   _____

   _____

5. My reward for achieving this is: _____

   _____

   _____

Conclusion

horough preparation is the most important factor in successful test taking. From the start of the semester implement appropriate strategies—actively participate in classes, labs, and review sessions; keep up with class notes and readings; and seek assistance when needed. As you increase your study time before an exam, develop review guides that combine and organize key information from your classes and readings. In addition, rehearse for the exam by practicing sample test questions and by teaching and questioning others. Finally, if you are experiencing excessive worry and nervousness, do practice recommended strategies to help reduce your anxiety.

Comprehension Check

evelop study cards for each chapter term on page 117. Write the term on the front of an index card and a brief explanation (in your own words) and example on the back.

Taking Tests

FOCUS QUESTION

Identify and describe strategies for taking each type of test—true/false, multiple choice, essay, and online.

CHAPTER TERMS

After reading this chapter, define (in your own words) and provide an example for each of the following terms:

- directive words
- qualifying words
- test-wiseness

Chapter 1	Chapter 2	Chapter 3	Chapter 4	Chapter 5	Chapter 6	Chapter 7	Chapter 8	Chapter 9
Academic Success	Managing Time	Being Productive	Active Listening	Reading Textbooks	Enhancing Memory	Test Preparation	**Taking Tests**	Continuing Success

Taking Tests: Two Essential Ingredients

Although test performance cannot be guaranteed, there are definite steps you can take to improve your test-taking skills. Two elements of successful test taking are:

1. Develop test-wiseness.
2. Review the test.

Develop Test-Wiseness

Test-wiseness refers to the skills and strategies related to *how to take* tests. It involves becoming familiar with and savvy about answering various types of questions (objective and essay) and formats of tests (hard-copy and online). When used in combination with (not as a substitute for) thorough, sound preparation, test-wiseness can noticeably improve your test-taking performance.

USE A FIVE-STEP COURSE OF ACTION

Step 1. Have supplies ready, including pen/pencils, extra paper (if allowed), and a watch to use for monitoring time. Assume that you will have to turn off your mobile phone and other telecommunication devices while taking the exam.

Step 2. Before looking at the test itself, use the back of the paper, the margins, or blank scratch paper to jot down details that are crammed into your head and you are afraid of forgetting. This step will (1) unburden your mind of those nagging details, and (2) provide you with a means to focus your attention immediately and involve yourself in the test-taking process.

Step 3. Prior to answering any questions, quickly look over the entire test and note the

- Length of the test.
- Types of questions and point value attached to each type.
- General difficulty level.

Also, carefully read the test instructions. Based on this information, strategize about how to approach the test given your time constraints. Generally, start with questions you can answer more readily or are worth more points; then tackle the difficult, time-consuming items.

"First, I skim through the test to see what it is like. By doing this step I sometimes notice clues that help me figure out questions. Then, I complete all the questions that I know. This helps to calm me down and boost my confidence." —NOAH

Critical Thinking Task

pause... *and reflect*

"Begin with objective questions, and then answer any essay questions."

Why is this strategy generally recommended for test taking? Do you agree with this suggestion? Why or why not?

Step 4. After completing questions you are sure of, go back and answer those questions that you left blank or put a question mark beside. At this point, you will be calmer and your mind will be clearer, allowing you to concentrate on how to answer the more difficult questions. Furthermore, now you might see clues to help you answer the questions you initially left blank.

Step 5. When you complete all items, go back and check for mistakes. Reread the test directions; you might discover that, in your haste, you misread directions the first time. Then, slowly reread each question. Use your *mouth*, though not your voice, to read and silently hear each question and answer. This technique will help you to check vigilantly for oversights and errors.

ONLINE COURSE WORK

For some online tests, you will be unable to do steps 3 through 5. Various online exams are set up so you *must* answer the questions in the order they appear on the screen. You cannot skip items and you cannot go back through the test. Therefore, before beginning an online test, confirm the setup; see if you can answer questions in the order of your choosing and if you can go back through the test before finishing.

WATCH FOR KEY WORDS

Pay attention to word choices in test questions. Look for key words or phrases in both objective and essay questions that pinpoint requirements for a correct answer. As an example, examine the following multiple-choice test question:

> "What is the main effect of the Hitler Jugend on events leading to the Holocaust?"

"Main effect" is the first key phrase; it implies that, although there may be many effects, your instructor is looking for the main, or foremost, effect. In addition, the word *effect* indicates you are searching for a cause-and-effect connection between ideas. In other words, when answering this question, consider how "_____ results in _____."

Other key words are the *terms* associated with the subject or topic. For this question, *Hitler Jugend* and *Holocaust* are the crucial terms that complete the cause-and-effect connection and thus are central to the correct answer.

Critical Thinking Task

pause... *and reflect*

For the following test questions, identify the key words. Note *why* each key word is important for providing the correct answer.

1. "What was the Final Solution, and who proposed it?"
2. "Number the events in the order in which they occurred."
3. "List three similarities and three differences between World War I and World War II."
4. "What statement best describes the long-term effects of the post–World War II tension between the United States and Russia?"
5. "Choose three statements that accurately describe how married life and family income were affected by the influx of women into the workforce after World War II."

LOOK FOR QUALIFYING WORDS

Qualifying words are words or phrases that moderate an extreme idea in a statement. They indicate that the statement's message is *not* a hard-and-fast rule. The presence of qualifying words suggests that exceptions, omissions, misstatements, or errors are possible. Consider a continuum (Figure 8.1) with "absolute" and "extreme" words at either end: absolutely "yes" at one end and absolutely "no" at the other. In between the ends are the vast majority of qualifying words indicating moderation, possible oversights, special conditions, and so on.

Qualifying words.

FIGURE   **8.1**

YES	IN-BETWEEN "QUALIFYING WORDS"	NO
definitely absolutely	usually somewhat maybe sometimes perhaps in my judgment	never have to
always certainly	most typically possibly generally to some extent in my opinion	none

Some messages *do* belong to one extreme or the other: "The earth *always* rotates on its axis" or "A human being *certainly* is not a reptile." Both of these statements contain extreme words and both happen to be true statements. However, most events fall somewhere in between the extreme ends:

- "It *definitely* rains in June." = FALSE
- "It *never* rains in June." = FALSE
- "It *usually* rains in June." = TRUE (This statement allows for the one June 50 years ago in which we had absolutely no rain.)

Many (not all) statements containing qualifying words happen to be true statements. Therefore, if you are not sure of the correct answer when reading a true/false statement on a test, use these tips:

- If qualifying words are present, the statement tends to be true.
- If absolute, extreme words are present, the statement often is false.

Remember: This method does *not* replace studying and knowing subject matter. Consider this a guide when you are stuck, not a hard-and-fast rule.

try it out!

Mark the following statements as either true or false. *Why* did you answer each item as you did? What *qualifying words* can you identify?

____ 1. In the year 2150, the projected worldwide life expectancy will be 86 years old.

____ 2. The world's crude-oil reserves likely will run out by the year 2063.

____ 3. The belief that smoking threatens a person's health is not linked to that person's beliefs about the severity of cancer.

____ 4. You should plan for some leisure activity during the day—everybody needs a break.

____ 5. Stress plays a role in all physical illness because of its effect on the immune system.

PRACTICE MULTIPLE-CHOICE QUESTIONS

Critical
Thinking
Task

Multiple-choice questions are the most popular type of test question, particularly in large introductory-level courses. Think of multiple-choice questions as a series of true/false statements: The lead-in clause or statement is combined with each option, forming a series of longer statements that are either true or false. Your task, as the test taker, is to choose the *best* true option. Here's a sample question:

1. In a test question, "compare" refers to
   A. A list of items.
   B. A relationship among items.
   C. Similarities among items.
   D. A + B.
   E. None of the above.
   F. All of the above.

By combining the lead-in clause with each of the six options, there are essentially six "true/false" statements for this one question:

A. In a test question, "compare" refers to a list of items.
B. In a test question, "compare" refers to a relationship among items.
C. In a test question, "compare" refers to similarities among items.
D. In a test question, "compare" refers to a list of items and a relationship among items.
E. ...and so on.

Note that options A through C are central to the answer because the remaining three options (D through F) are various combinations of the first three choices. Thus you should focus on the first three statements (A through C) and identify each as being true *or* false:

A. In a test question, "compare" refers to a list of items. [*This statement is false*.]
B. In a test question, "compare" refers to a relationship among items. [*This statement is true because a relationship or connection does exist in a comparison*.]
C. In a test question, "compare" refers to similarities among items. [*This statement is definitely true because "compare" means "like" or "similar to."*]

You are searching for the *one* true statement as the answer. Given that you identified two true statements, look at the remaining three choices to see if "B + C" is an option. Only "A + B" is presented, and you can eliminate this option (D) because it is a false statement. Likewise, both options E and F have to be false (because *at least one* but *not all* of statements A through C are true). Thus choose option C as your *best answer*.

In summary, viewing multiple-choice items as a series of true/false statements can simplify your test-taking approach, especially when multiple combinations are present as options. As you read the lead-in clause with each option, write "T" or "F" beside that option, with the goal of ultimately choosing the one "T." If you have more than one "T," then look at the combinations, ultimately choosing the *best* option as your answer.

Strategies for choosing which option is best and which options can be eliminated are summarized next. If you are not sure of the so-called best answer on a test, these strategies will help you to make *informed guesses*:

1. Select the more *specific and inclusive* choice (this often is the longest option). Eliminate extremely general options.

2. Eliminate *grammatical mismatches* when combining the lead-in clause with an option, such as a plural subject with a singular verb.

   Example for strategies 1 and 2: When setting career goals for yourself
   A. Evaluate your options, including personal, emotional, and monetary costs. [*includes more specific information*]
   B. Career goals can be determined later. [*too general; not grammatically correct when read with the lead-in clause*]
   Option A is the best answer.

3. Select an option that is *similar in format* to others, such as containing repeated terms, a similar structure, or the same word pattern.

   Example for strategy 3: Research demonstrates that people who practice deep muscle relaxation
   A. Exhibit decreases in psychological well-being.
   B. Show little difference from the control group.
   C. Exhibit increases in psychological well-being. [*options A and C are similar in format*]
   Option C is the best answer.

4. If a *word or phrase is repeated* throughout the test, it tends to be part of a true option at some point.

5. Focus on *familiar terminology* as possible true options. Instructors sometimes use vocabulary that does not relate to the subject matter; if you have never seen the term before, consider it a false option.

   Example for strategies 4 and 5: Deep breathing consists of
   A. Adrenaline flowing through your body.
   B. Full, even breaths originating in your abdomen. [*repetition of "breathing" and "breaths"*]
   Option B is the best answer.

6. When "*not*" is part of the lead-in clause, eliminate "not" when reading the statement and then search for the false option.

   Example for strategy 6: Which is <u>not</u> a benefit of meditation? *is changed to* Which <u>is</u> a benefit of meditation?
   A. Improved mood. [*true*]
   B. Increased heart rate. [*false*]
   C. Increased energy. [*true*]
      Option B is the best answer.

7. Be aware of *qualifying words,* often indicating true statements, and *absolute words,* often indicating false statements (see Figure 8.1).

   Example for strategy 7: Deep breathing
   A. Tends to elevate moods. [*"tends to" is a qualifying phrase*]
   B. Definitely decreases depression and anxiety. [*"definitely" is an absolute word*]
      Option A is the best answer.

8. A *middle option* tends to be correct more often than are beginning or ending options, especially when presented with a range of numbers.

   Example for strategy 8: College students should have how many hours of sleep per night?
   A. 6–8 hours
   B. 7–9 hours
   C. 9–11 hours
      Option B is the best answer.

9. "All of the above" is more often true; "none of the above" is more often false. Instructors prefer testing students about what is *present* on paper ("all of the above"), as opposed to what is *missing* ("none of the above").

10. If you are not sure, use your background knowledge, experiences, and common sense!

    Example for strategies 9 and 10: You can reduce levels of stress with
    A. Physical exercise. [*true*]
    B. The support of friends or family. [*true*]
    C. A forgiving and hopeful frame of mind. [*not sure, but I'll consider it "true" because it makes sense*]
    D. All the above.
    E. None of the above.
       Option D is the best answer.

11. If you are *not* being penalized for wrong answers, then don't leave an answer blank. You might as well *guess*!

try it out!

Critical
thinking
task

What is the *best* answer for each of the following multiple-choice questions? Write your reasons for selecting or eliminating options, using the previous list of strategies.

1. "Soy isolate" is
   A. A white powdered food that is 90% protein.
   B. A white powdered food that is 90% carbohydrate.
   C. A chemical compound used in kitchen utensils.
   D. A + B

2. The characteristics of "microtubules" include:
   A. They have a shape of straight, hollow tubes.
   B. They have a shape of solid rods.
   C. They have a size of approximately 25 nm.
   D. A + B
   E. A + C
   F. All of the above.

3. Which operations are associated with the information-processing model of memory?
   A. Input, storage, and retrieval
   B. Input, rehearsal, and output
   C. Process, storage, and recall
   D. Encode, consolidate, and retrieval

4. In one research study, college students had more accurate memories:
   A. The students needed repetitive coaxing.
   B. The students did not have more accurate memories.
   C. When they exhibited abnormal disorders.
   D. When they had high blood sugar levels.

5. An instructional method that does *not* enhance creative thought is
   A. Establishing preset rules.
   B. Establishing collaborative learning groups.
   C. Using illustrations.

> ### ONLINE COURSE WORK
>
> As noted in Chapter 7, do rehearse taking online tests. This practice will help to increase your pacing and speed, decision-making, and overall familiarity with the online format. Also, be prepared for extra security measures, especially if taking the test in a campus testing center. Protocols such as individual scan codes, assigned seating, and removal of jackets and mobile phones can be intimidating but are standard at many college testing sites.

PRACTICE ESSAY QUESTIONS

Critical Thinking Task

Expect to encounter essay questions, especially in social science courses and in smaller higher-level courses. Instructors often expect students to exhibit higher-level thought processes when answering essay questions.

Have a clear understanding of **directive words,** those specific words in essay questions signaling *what the instructor expects in your answer*. Directive words orient you as to what to include and *how to organize* your answer. Test your knowledge of directive words by completing the second column in Figure 8.2. (The first item is done for you.)

The following steps provide a general guideline to assist you with successfully completing essay-type test items.

Step 1. Be clear on the *type* and *length* of answer that your instructor expects.

- For a short-answer essay question, expect to write one to two paragraphs for your answer.
- For a longer essay question, write several substantial paragraphs, amounting to one or more pages in length.

Step 2. Read the question and *jot down your immediate thoughts*. What terms and ideas do you associate with the question?

Step 3. Circle or underline *key words* within the question, including *directive words*, such as those in Figure 8.2, and words or terms *linked* to the topic.

Step 4. Reflect on the *ideas* that will adequately answer the question, writing a draft as you move along:

- Decide about the main idea of your answer; then draft a *thesis statement* representing this main idea. Use key words in the question to form your introductory statement.

Directive words.   FIGURE **8.2**

Directive Words	What I Should Include in My Answer
Compare	***similarities*** *between/among ideas; how "things" are* **alike** *(can also include differences)*
Contrast	
Critique	
Define	
Describe	
Discuss	
Evaluate	
Explain	
Identify	
Illustrate	
Justify	
List	
Relate	
Summarize	
Trace	

- Decide about appropriate *supporting ideas* and how to *organize* these ideas. What information will you include that explains, supports, or relates to your thesis?
- Decide about *specific evidence* or *examples* that make your answer more accurate and precise.
- Refer back to your immediate jottings (step 2). Should you add any of these initial thoughts to your draft?

Step 5. Carefully read through your draft, mouthing the words so you will see and hear your ideas.

- Does your answer make sense? Are you answering completely?
- Are you accurate yet concise? (Do not pad your answer with excessive details—consider the impression your answer will make on your instructor, who will be reading a stack of similar answers!)
- Do your ideas flow smoothly—that is, are you connecting thoughts to increase the fluency of ideas?

Step 6. Read your answer backward so you concentrate on each word and catch any spelling errors.

Figure 8.3 shows a question, a breakdown of the six-step process, and a sample answer.

try *it out!*

Critical
Thinking
Task

For practice and as part of the chapter comprehension check, write a short essay answer for the focus question at the beginning of this chapter. Then critique your answer using the following criteria:

- Do you have a clearly written thesis statement that begins your answer? Establish your main idea at the start of your essay. This will focus your thoughts as the writer and your instructor's thoughts as the reader. When grading the tests, your instructor will be looking for key ideas in each of many essay exams. Therefore, make sure your key ideas are clearly stated at the start of your essay.
- Have you provided supporting ideas for your thesis statement? Include adequate and accurate details (examples, evidence, characteristics, explanations) to strengthen your ideas.
- Are your ideas organized?
- Have you made appropriate transitions between ideas? Include words such as *also, in addition, for example, such as, on the other hand, first, second, then, next, therefore, as a result, in summary*.
- Have you included a simple, tightly worded conclusion? End with a simple rewording of the thesis.
- Is your answer clearly written without padding (extra words or ideas)?
- Is the essay easy to read and understand?
- Is your essay free of all spelling and grammar errors?

Remember: Your instructor will be reading many answers to the same question. Therefore, strive to create an answer that correctly and distinctively illustrates your understanding of the subject matter.

Sample essay question and answer.   FIGURE **8.3**

"Compare and contrast the leadership of Franklin D. Roosevelt and Adolf Hitler."

Step 1: The instructor expects some detail and/or examples to explain the main idea; length is approximately two to three paragraphs, 250–300 words.

Step 2: Immediate thoughts that the student associated with the question:

> FDR—U. S. president; well liked, especially by lower class; New Deal to reverse Depression and poverty; optimistic; bad economic times.

> Hitler—Germany; dictator; pessimistic; used Jews and others as scapegoats; bad economic times; well liked.

Step 3: Identify key words in the question.
"Compare and *contrast* the leadership of Franklin D. *Roosevelt* and Adolf *Hitler."*

Step 4: (A) Create a thesis statement:
Roosevelt and Hitler were important world leaders but had different backgrounds and actions.

(B) Identify supporting ideas with specifics in chronological order:

- FDR born wealthy; Hitler born to civil servants.
- Both school dropouts.
- American and German people's resentment—Hoover administration (U. S.) and Weimar Republic (Germany).
- Initially, both not considered capable of leading.
- Democracy vs. dictatorship.
- Both had psychological influence on the public, emphasizing the current economic hardships and gaining popularity/support from the lower class.
- Roosevelt sympathized with the poor; he was honest about the present economic hardships but optimistic about the future—hope and confidence.
- Hitler emphasized hatred and violence against Jews, communists, the wealthy, and minorities, focusing on fears and projecting images of strength, power, and hard work.
- Both used radio for propaganda: Roosevelt—weekly "Fireside Chat" for intimate connections with people. Hitler mandated radios; broadcast explosive speeches in front of cheering crowds.

(C) Identify connecting thoughts for "compare" and "contrast": similar; opposing; although; both; on the other hand; whereas; in contrast; different from; and; furthermore.

(continued)

FIGURE **8.3** *Continued.*

After doing **Step 5** (carefully reading through the draft and revising) and **Step 6** (reading backward to catch spelling errors), the student completed the answer:

Completed Answer

Franklin Roosevelt and Adolf Hitler were significant world leaders who had both similar and opposing backgrounds, personality characteristics, and leadership styles. Roosevelt was born to a wealthy and influential political family of New York. On the other hand, Hitler was a child of a minor civil servant in Austria; he adopted Germany as his homeland later on. Both shared experiences as school dropouts and spent some perplexing years before they found their niche in politics.

Their rise to power in the 1933 elections was a result of resentment by the American and German people—resentment against the Hoover administration in the United States and against the Weimar Republic in Germany. Initially, both leaders were not considered to be capable of their new positions. Under Hitler, a one-party dictatorship was established, whereas Roosevelt led a democratic government in the United States.

Both Hitler and Roosevelt had great psychological influence on the public. Both emphasized the current economic hardships, gaining popularity and support from the lower class of their countries. Roosevelt sympathized with the poor; he was honest about the present economic hardships but optimistic about the future.

He infused the American people with hope and confidence. In contrast, Hitler's popularity was built on a platform of hatred and violence against Jews, communists, the wealthy, and other minorities. He focused on people's fears, projecting images of strength, power, and hard work to counter those fears.

Furthermore, both leaders masterfully used the radio for broadcasting propaganda. Roosevelt hosted a weekly "Fireside Chat" to make intimate connections with the American people. Hitler mandated that all households in Germany have radios. Different from Roosevelt in style, only Hitler's explosive speeches in front of cheering crowds were broadcast to the German people.

In summary, Franklin Roosevelt and Adolf Hitler were influential world leaders who, though outwardly different, shared a number of leadership traits.

[Contributed by Yue Ying Zhang]

Review the Test

The often-heard adage is true: You *do* learn from your mistakes! Receiving a test score is not enough; go back over test items, especially those that you answered incorrectly, in an effort to improve your performance on the next test for that course. If your instructor does not pass back the exam or does not use class time to review common errors, make an appointment to review your test during the instructor's office hours. Sometimes instructors allow students to go over test material with a graduate teaching assistant, trusted tutor, or a faculty member specializing in learning skills.

ONLINE COURSE WORK

Take advantage of your instructor's online, email, and/or video-conferencing office hours to discuss the exam. If possible, ask for an appointment to review the test and talk about your preparation techniques. In your messages to your instructor, always use polite, formal language—that is, complete sentences with correct grammar, capitalization, punctuation, and spelling. Also, identify yourself by using your full name and student identification number, as well as the course title and section number.

When reviewing your test, study how the test items are constructed. Most test items require more than pure memorization. Instead, you are required to relate ideas, apply concepts, distinguish similarities or differences, identify effects, or examine case studies. Taking the time and effort to review a previous test carefully is a valuable strategy in preparing you for the next test. As you continue to take class notes, read, and do assignments for a course, think ahead to the next exam: What will you need to know and how will the information be presented on the test?

In addition, when reviewing a test pay special attention to your errors. Generally, mistakes are related to one or more of the following causes:

- **Insufficient preparation:** not understanding and remembering the content well enough.
- **Inadequate test-taking skills:** not knowing how to approach the particular types of questions on the test. Or, in the case of online tests, being unfamiliar with the technology or uncomfortable with the setup of the exam.
- **Extreme anxiety:** a reaction that interferes with your test performance.

As you examine what you did right and wrong on the test, consider (1) what you can do to prepare yourself better for the next test (see Chapter 7), and (2) where you can go or who you can see for added support and guidance (your instructor, study group, learning center, tutorial center, computer lab, or counseling center).

Critical
Thinking
Task

pause.... *and reflect*

Identify a recent test that you will review, whether in class, out of class, or online. Spend time carefully examining your responses. Do you recognize patterns of how you tend to approach and answer questions? *Why* did you make errors on this test (insufficient preparation, inadequate test-taking skills, or extreme anxiety)? *How* will you prepare for your next test?

Conclusion

A myriad of factors intertwine to produce successful test results. The following items provide a summary of strategies for preparing for and taking quizzes and exams. As test time approaches for each subject, use these questions as reminders of strategies that will provide you with the advantages associated with successful test results.

SUMMARY OF TEST-TAKING STRATEGIES

ARE YOU SUFFICIENTLY PREPARED?

- Have you kept up with week-to-week class work, assignments, and regular review?
- Have you added extra study time the week before the exam?
- Have you reviewed and consolidated class notes and readings into a study guide?
- Have you practiced answering test questions?
- Have you taught and thoroughly discussed the subject matter with others?

IS YOUR TEST ANXIETY AT A MANAGEABLE LEVEL?

- Have you practiced strategies to reduce your anxiety in stressful test situations?
- Do you know how to calm both your thoughts and your physical reactions to a test?

ARE YOU KNOWLEDGEABLE ABOUT *HOW* TO TAKE TESTS?

- Do you know the steps to follow when taking the test?
  - At the start do you get an *overview* of the test: (1) read the directions thoroughly; (2) note the number, type, and point value of questions; and (3) develop a strategy for tackling the test within designated time constraints?
  - After finishing a test, do you go back and review your answers, looking for careless errors? Do you move your mouth from word to word? Or do you move your finger from word to word?
- Have you practiced identifying key words in questions, including terms and qualifying words?
- Have you practiced how to answer multiple-choice questions—that is, how to eliminate incorrect options while choosing the best option?
- Have you practiced writing essays that answer the question correctly and clearly?
- Have you practiced taking online tests?

HAVE YOU REVIEWED YOUR CORRECTED TEST?

- Do you have a clear understanding of why answers are correct or incorrect?
- Did you discover why you made your errors?
- Have you considered ways to prepare yourself better for the next test?

try it out!

Learning Strategies and Taking Tests

1. Identify a test that is coming up in one of your courses.
2. Refer to the Summary of Test-Taking Strategies (pp. 152–153) and choose one of the test-taking strategies that you will implement for this test.
3. Write a Personal Action Statement.
4. **Assess Your Success** after taking the test:
   - Did you follow through and reward yourself accordingly? Explain.
   - Did the hurdle materialize and did you manage it effectively?
   - What other changes do you want to make before your next quiz or exam?

Your Personal Action Statement

Identify an upcoming test: _____

1. I will: _____

   _____

   _____

2. My greatest hurdle to achieving this is: _____

   _____

   _____

3. I will eliminate this hurdle by: _____

   _____

   _____

4. My time frame for achieving this is: _____

   _____

   _____

5. My reward for achieving this is: _____

   _____

Comprehension Check

eturn to the beginning of the chapter; define the chapter terms in your own words and provide an example of each.

CHAPTER 9

Continuing Your Academic Success
A REVIEW

FOCUS QUESTION

How can I continue to apply, monitor, and change my system of study?

CHAPTER TERM

After reading this chapter, define (in your own words) and provide an example for the following term:

- Personal Action Plan

As outlined in Chapter 1, your success in college depends on a combination of factors: the learning strategies you choose to apply in and out of class, as well as your attitude and commitment to working hard and achieving your goals. The previous chapters provided a medley of strategies to build and strengthen your system of study. However, keep in mind that an effective system of study is not constant. Each term you will face a different set of academic assignments, personal demands, and social desires. At that point, do a personal appraisal of what strategies do and do not work for you. Adjust your study practices as needed to accommodate your varying courses, instructors, and requirements. The following suggestions will help you select and accomplish those adjustments and, as a result, continue on your path of academic success.

Your Personal Action Plan

For each major topic in the text, you chose a specific strategy to apply and then assess by means of a Personal Action Statement. The accumulation of your Personal Action Statements provides an overview of what you have put into practice this semester: what strategies you have used and how successful they have been for you. Now is the time to review your Personal Action Statements with the intent of combining and modifying them to create a global **Personal Action Plan,** an overview of learning behaviors and attitudes that are effective for you.

try it out!

Create a blueprint for your Personal Action Plan. Complete the three columns in Figure 9.1 to create a personal profile of your study system.

Critical
Thinking
Task

1. **What I Do Well.** Note specific practices that have become a vital part of your learning and study methods.
2. **What I Will Change Now.** Jot down a definite strategy that likely will benefit you and that you will put into practice. *Remember*: You are much more prone to follow through if you write down your intention.
3. **How Effective?** This column provides a quick means for follow-up. Note how effective or successful you were with each strategy that you tried.

My Personal Action Plan.

FIGURE   9.1

	What I Do Well	What I Will Change Now	How Effective?
1. Managing my time • Use schedule, planner, and calendar. • Balance academic, personal, and social demands. • Reduce procrastination.			
2. Maximizing productivity • Choose a suitable study location. • Organize self, space, and materials. • Minimize distractions. • Reduce stress.			
3. Selective and attentive listening in class or via Web • Create clear, correct, concise notes. • Review notes and create study guides.			
4. Understanding reading assignments • Preview before. • Check for understanding while reading. • Create study guides for review.			
5. Increase learning and memory • Get adequate sleep. • Review immediately. • Study regularly. • Organize/categorize. • Use my senses. • Associate. • Study with others.			
6. Preparing well for tests • Stay current with work. • Make review guides. • Rehearse. • Manage worry and anxiety.			

(continued)

FIGURE **9.1** *Continued.*			

• Practice reading and answering test items:
  • True/False
  • Multiple Choice
  • Essay
  • Online			

7. Taking tests successfully
  • Develop test-wisensess.
  • Review the test afterward.			

Conclusion

The following checklist of items was presented in the Conclusion of Chapter 1. Review the checklist, and determine to how many of the items you can confidently answer yes. Use the checklist periodically to keep yourself on the track to academic success.

Critical Thinking Task

○ 1. Are you clear about why you are attending college and what you expect to get out of college?

○ 2. Do you know what each instructor expects of you? Have you read—and reread—each syllabus and met with the instructor? Have you regularly attended review sessions?

○ 3. Are you managing your time wisely? Are you assessing your priorities periodically and establishing a routine that balances your academic, personal, and social/leisure demands?

○ 4. Are you using effective methods of study for each course?

○ 5. Are you involving yourself in college life by participating in campus activities?

○ 6. Are you avoiding these hazards?
  • Mishandling of your personal freedom and time.
  • Misuse of alcohol and drugs.
  • Mishandling of your personal health.
  • Mishandling of your best interests.

As you monitor and adjust how you study and learn, note the feelings of self-confidence and empowerment that accompany your development as a student and a learner. The skills, attitudes, and self-knowledge that lead you toward success in college will also serve you well beyond college as you fulfill your career aspirations and personal goals.

Index